WHERE SEAGULLS DARE

WHERE SEAGULLS DARE

THE INSIDER GUIDE TO THE BEST OF THE HIGHLANDS AND ISLANDS

IAIN MACDONALD

&

RAB MACWILLIAM

KESSOCK BOOKS

First published in Great Britain by
Kessock Books 2016

A CIP catalogue record for this book is available from the British Library
ISBN 978-0-9930296-3-9

Designed by Audiografix

Printed and bound in Great Britain by CPI Group (UK),
Croydon, CR40 4YY

CONTENTS

ABOUT THE AUTHORS

Iain MacDonald was born and brought up in Stornoway on the island of Lewis. Educated at the Nicolson Institute, he emigrated to mainland Scotland, where he worked as a door-to-door salesman, a labourer and an occasional zoo keeper, which taught him how to deal with politicians.

He began his journalistic career in Aberdeen, before moving to Inverness, where he worked as a reporter, as well as writing a weekly music column. He became editor of the late lamented *Football Times* in the last days of hot-metal printing, and, indeed, of the *Football Times*. He joined the BBC's Radio Highland in 1978 and avoided the sack for 35 years. His work took him to many parts of Europe, the USA and to Westminster, as well as longer spells with BBC Scotland in Glasgow. None of these was as exotic as Wick.

He was chairman of the National Union of Journalists' Highlands and Islands branch and was twice named Journalist of the Year in the Highlands and Islands Media awards. His other occupations have included goalkeeping and running after a dog. He is reasonably sober and can be trusted with small amounts of money.

Rab MacWilliam was born in Inverness and attended the Crown Primary School and Inverness Royal Academy. Between 1969 and 1975 he studied at the Universities of Edinburgh and Essex, eventually graduating from the latter with a degree in Politics.

He moved permanently to London in the mid-1970s, and worked for over twenty years in book publishing as a commissioning editor and publisher with Hutchinson, Penguin, Hamlyn and others, before he quit corporate life in 1996. Since then he has been a freelance editor, writer and author. In 1999 he established *N16 Magazine* in Stoke Newington and was Editor of the mag for twelve years.

In 2014 he became Publishing Director of Kessock Books, for whom he has written two books – *Snow on the Ben* and *Views from the Ben* – as well as the text for his sister-in-law Merrill's collection of drawings, *Moments in Time*.

His diversions include watching football, playing acoustic guitar, listening to old folk-blues albums, remaining sober, and making life difficult for himself, although not all at the same time.

INTRODUCTION

Although your luggage may at this moment be trundling forlornly around a baggage carousel somewhere in the depths of Frankfurt Airport, or you're sitting in a car on a bendy road behind an interminably slow-moving trail of caravans, at least you have finally reached your destination: the Highlands and Islands of Scotland.

This may be your first glimpse of this land of myth and mountains, of fantasy and fable, or you may have been here before. Whichever the case, what you almost certainly want to discover is where to find the most interesting and intriguing places, their history and culture, and how best to enjoy them. Also, some insider knowledge and insights will help you understand and appreciate their different and special environments.

There is a great deal of information available for tourists and visitors to this unique region, and there are several well-researched publications and websites which will help you in your quest. However, there are also many other sources which offer out-of-date listings, self-seeking hyperbole, misleading myths, romantic but error-strewn histories, tedious and unhelpful information, and much more besides.

We're guessing here, but you'd probably welcome an entertaining, amusing read, as well as an informative guide to some of the Highland's most fascinating regions: one which also contains anecdotes, local opinions and knowledge which will provide you with a fresh and vivid understanding of this unique part of Britain.

Where Seagulls Dare, then, is the book for you. But why 'seagulls', you may ask? Well, it's clearly a pun on the title of Alistair Maclean's book and the subsequent film. But it's also a metaphor which suggests that you have now arrived at the edge of town and are concerned about venturing into another, quite different land: by some accounts, an alien, rugged and unknown place, a territory in which even the most streetwise of urban survivalists – a seagull, perhaps – would not feel comfortable. Your concerns, however, are misplaced. With this book as your companion, you will discover some of the most diverse, beautiful and welcoming settlements and landscapes in Europe. And perhaps a few foolhardy seagulls.

The book has been written and compiled by two native, born-and-bred Highlanders – one a journalist and broadcaster, the other a professional writer and editor – who have been friends for over forty years. They have between them travelled all over the Highlands and Islands, and they are well acquainted with all aspects of Highland life and culture in its many manifestations, both high and low life.

We share a mild distaste for the image of the Highlands as some 'land o' the shinin' heather', swirlingly-kilted, tartan-bedecked Gaelic paradise of winsome 'wee lassies', brawny, 'laddies' and forelock-tugging, tweedy old crofters, all bowing in deference to the saintly Bonny Prince Charlie, while the peat smoke curls from the crooked chimneys of the villages as the sun sets over the ancient castles and serene mountains of this proud land.

We exaggerate, of course, but do so only in order to make a serious point. Although in many areas – particularly in and around Assynt, Torridon, the Great Glen, Skye and Kintail – the scenery is undeniably breathtaking in its awesome splendour, this is a land of contrasts. The Highlands is an ever-changing, multi-faceted and diverse area. It can indeed approximate to the 'land o' the shinin' heather' vision, but there is so much more here to excite one's attention and interest.

In this special part of Britain you will find centuries-old fishing hamlets nestling in the shadow of huge oilrig fabrication yards; long sandy beaches stretching for miles and served by small holiday resorts; large expanses of sparsely inhabited, peaty moorland, such as the Flow Country of Caithness and Sutherland, the largest such formation in Europe; large fish-processing factories dwarfing 19th- century small harbours; bustling market towns such as Dingwall and Portree; the brooding, menacing old fortified keeps of Castle Urquhart and Eilean Donan; the ostentatious, grandiose follies of Dunrobin and Carbisdale Castles; whisky distilleries next to the salmon-rich rivers, fertile soil and agricultural richness of the Beauly and west Nairnshire farmlands; and the metropolitan, fast-expanding 'Highland Capital' city of Inverness.

There are also elegant old tower houses and Scottish Baronial residences standing proudly among acres of beech, spruce and fir trees; some of the world's oldest and most respected golf courses; abandoned old buildings and dwelling houses, a legacy of the devastating Highland Clearances; standing stones and circles dating back to pre-Pictish and pre-Celtic eras; sheltered villages huddled under the protective hills and mountains surrounding the deep sea lochs of the West Coast; an abundance of rare wildlife and bird species unmatched anywhere in Britain; and there is so much else to discover. The Highlands is an outstandingly beautiful region, but is also far more complex, intriguing and multi-layered than is generally realised.

Where Seagulls Dare contains illuminating, entertaining and well-informed descriptions of, and personal insights into, twenty-five special places which we have detailed in the List of Contents: places which we feel are essential to visit in order to understand the true, varied nature of the Highlands. We make no claim to be entirely comprehensive but, with our blend of fact, history, anecdote, humour and often quirky perspectives, we offer you a view of the Highlands and Islands which is rarely found in more conventional guidebooks.

Where Seagulls Dare will provide you with a full appreciation of the elusive essence and dramatic nature of Europe's most strikingly original region. We very much hope you enjoy reading this book.

Iain MacDonald and Rab MacWilliam

Acknowledgements

We'd like to thank a number of people for their help when we were writing *Where Seagulls Dare*. Above all, our partners, Beech and Judi, encouraged us and tolerated our daft phone calls, unsocial hours, panicking, cursing and a good deal more. Many thanks to you both. We are also grateful for the support, enthusiasm and insights provided by everyone at Kessock Books, and also, on individual areas, from a good number of friends and local residents. There are too many people to name here but you know who you are.

Specifically, our gratitude goes to Merrill MacWilliam, who is a Kessock Books director and author, Rab's sister-in-law and an exceptionally talented artist, who allowed us to use several of her drawings in the text to complement the photographs, which were mainly taken by Iain. Ewen Weatherspoon provided the photos of Brora, Dingwall and the Cuillins (to illustrate Dunvegan), and we thank him for this.

About the cover photographer

John Paul, a professional photographer since 1982, has been published widely throughout the world from his Inverness base. Trained as commercial photographer in Glasgow, John went on to work for national newspapers and magazines covering major news throughout the 1980s and 1990s. During that time, he was named as Journalist of the Year for the Highlands and Islands. These days, he concentrates on projects in the whisky, food and fashion industries. John lives in Inverness with Dutch partner Jannet, and two children. johnpaul.photography

We appreciate the spirit of Highland generosity in which everyone's assistance was volunteered, and please be assured that we will repay you in kind when next we meet.

A brief note on the layout of the text

The authors come from rather different writing backgrounds: Iain is a radio and newspaper journalist and broadcaster while Rab is a book and magazine editor and publisher. We are both born-and-bred Highlanders – Iain from Stornoway and Rab from Inverness – and we have each travelled widely across the Highlands and Islands. We have known each other for over forty years, and our world view generally, and of the Highlands in particular, is similar.

Nevertheless, it is difficult to write a book of this nature as if it were in effect by one writer, particularly as Iain lives in Inverness and Rab in London. Therefore, we decided to separate our comments, with Rab's contribution in conventional text and Iain's in italicised type. We also felt that such a distinction would permit both of us to express our views in our individual ways, and that the reader might find such a distinction to be of more interest. We refer to each other's articles in the text when we think the reader may find this helpful.

There is a small element of repetition in the book. This is deliberate, and is either for purposes of emphasis and/or because the reader may benefit from a reminder. And, as the Highlands is a relatively small region, there are occasional geographical overlaps. But we did our best to avoid this, and we much enjoyed working together on the book.

MAP OF SCOTTISH
HIGHLANDS AND ISLANDS

ASSYNT:
THE ANCIENT MOUNTAINS

Of the many wild and remote areas in Europe, there are very few which can compare with the brooding solitude and spectacular splendour of Assynt in the Western Highlands of Scotland.

Assynt lies on the west of the county of Sutherland. The jagged coastline and deep sea lochs, fast-flowing rivers, steep valleys, innumerable lochans, scattered human settlements, dense woodlands, rich diversity of wildlife, windswept moorlands and, above all, the astonishing, ancient mountains which proudly dominate this extraordinary landscape are awe-inspiring. It is no surprise that Assynt has been designated as the North-West Highlands Geopark.

The origin of the name 'Assynt' is obscure but probably derives from the Old Norse 'ass' meaning a 'rocky ridge', while in Gaelic it's called 'Asainte'. Assynt is normally regarded as the area bounded by Point of Stoer (the tip of the peninsula on the coastal road north of Lochinver), Kylesku (on the A894 where Loch a Charn Bhain meets Loch Glendhu), Ledmore (a small inland village to the south) and Inverkirkaig (a coastal settlement just south of Lochinver).

Assynt has been settled since around 5000 BC. The remains of monumental houses, crannogs, placenames and vitrified buildings testify to its Pictish, Gaelic and Norse influences over the centuries. After the departure of the Norsemen, King David II gave the lands of Assynt to the Macleods of Lewis in an attempt to secure the Western clans' allegiance to Scotland. By the early 17th century the MacKenzies had ousted the MacLeods, and the former clan were formally granted Assynt after the Restoration of the English monarchy. Then the Sutherland family bought Assynt in 1757.

When you visit the North of Scotland, you absolutely should not miss the opportunity to head north-west to this rugged Hielan' wilderness. The hills and mountains of Assynt are some of the oldest in the world. They are unimaginably ancient in their origin: I'd tell you how old they are, but you probably wouldn't believe me. They are formed of Lewisian gneiss, often overlaid with Torridian sandstone, and a few are 'Munros' (over 3,000 feet high) with several being 'Corbetts' (2,500-3,000 feet). ('Munros', incidentally, are named after Sir Hugh Munro who compiled the first listing in 1891.)

A geologist friend of mine informs me that the Assynt area is world-renowned in the science of geology. A phenomenon known as the 'Moine Thrust' runs from Loch Eriboll on the North Highland coast close to Cape Wrath, through Assynt and down to the Sleat Peninsula on Skye. Its discovery was a milestone in the study of earth science, as it helped to prove the theory of plate tectonics. Knockan Crag, just south of Ledmore in Assynt, is of the highest importance to geologists for just this reason.

Probably the most distinctive of the mountains in Assynt is Suilven (deriving from the Old Norse for 'the pillar', its name in Gaelic being 'S'ula Bheinn'), an almost vertical mountain whose sugar-loaf-shaped summit of Caisteal Liath ('grey castle') dominates the nearby town of Lochinver. Close by is Canisp (Old Norse for 'white mountain') and, overlooking Loch Assynt, is Quinaig (from the Gaelic 'A' Chuineag' or 'milking pail'), a Y-shaped range of three peaks. To the east is Ben More Assynt (from the Gaelic 'beinn mhor Asaint': 'the big mountain of Assynt') which, at 3274 feet, is the highest point in the county of Sutherland.

Further south you'll find Cul Mor (Gaelic for 'small back') and the relatively small Stac Polly (the English form of the Gaelic 'Stac Pollaidh', although the origin of its name is from the Old Norse 'Stakkr Polla': 'pinnacle of the pool river'). And there are plenty more which insist on exploration.

The remarkable geological structure of Assynt can also be discovered underground. Five miles south of Inchnadamph ('Inis nan Damh': 'meadow of the stags'), a village on the eastern end of Loch Assynt, there exists a cave known as Uamh an Claonaite ('cave of the sloping rock') which, at 1.8 miles long and 360 feet deep, is easily the longest cave in Scotland and a potholer's paradise.

The area's wildlife is varied and bounteous. Herds of red deer roam the valleys and hills while stags warily strut their stuff in the event of potential interference from rivals. Above them reel shadows of indignant eagles, curlews, Arctic terns, hooded crows and similar other haughty winged lords of the sky. A survey revealed that 215 species of birds have been recorded in recent years in the

Assynt area. Salmon and otters populate the many burns and rivers, and from observation points on the coast one can observe whales, dolphins, porpoises and seals cavorting in The Minch, the stormy expanse of sea which separates mainland Scotland from the Outer Hebrides.

There are several small villages and settlements in the Assynt area, the largest being Lochinver on the coast, situated where the A837 comes to a sudden halt. Lochinver is Scotland's second-largest fishing port, and many of the fishing boats come up The Minch from France and Spain. The harbour, to the south of the town, was rebuilt in 1990 and is the busiest in the Highland Council region.

The Culag and Inverlodge hotels afford wide-ranging views of Loch Inver, the former having been built in 1873 as a shooting lodge and refurbished after a fire in 1939. The latter, along with a few other establishments in Lochinver and its neighbour Baddidarrach, has in recent years become internationally recognised for the high quality of the cuisine on offer.

On the north side of Lochinver are the main shopping street, the Assynt Visitor Centre opened in 1995, a war memorial and the Highland Stoneware Pottery. The Culag Woods, with abundant plant life and a heronry, are natural woodland around the town and are managed by a community trust. Further north there are several interesting villages, including Clashmore, Stoer and Drumbeg. The looping single-track road, the B869, around the peninsula from Lochinver to Kylestrome is not for the faint-hearted, with its gradient rising in places to 25%.

Assynt, however, suffered badly from The Clearances, which began here in 1812 when the area was divided into five large sheep farms. This incited a crofters' rebellion, but by 1821 over 160 families had been evicted. The Duke and Duchess of Sutherland were particularly cruel exponents of this new land-use system. By 1830 only 11 families remained in an area which had once been home to hundreds of tenants.

Sporadic crofter revolts persisted until the late 19th century, when in 1887 and 1888, some tenants took violent possession of their lands and the Duke called in gunboats to crush the uprising. All the tenants were arrested except for one Hugh Kerr (hailed locally as 'the modern Rob Roy') who avoided capture for two months. Good man. When The Clearances gradually died away, the previously commonly-held lands were divided into family-owned crofts, with each family having its own plot. But the system offered only bare subsistence, and crofting had to be supplemented by other forms of employment. So, as they had done for many years, people continued to emigrate to North America, and the local population gradually declined. However, as the 20th century progressed, the Highland economy slowly improved, helped by the arrival of hydroelectric power, the rise in tourism and, crucially, the discovery and exploitation of North Sea oil.

Although much of the Highlands today remains in private hands, one hopes that the Scottish government will make every effort to bring the land back to the people for community use. Recent developments indicate that this is perfectly possible, as is reflected in the changing nature of land ownership in parts of the Highlands. In this crucial re-assumption of the people's land, Assynt has played a leading role.

'Now we have the land'

The Assynt Crofters' Estate is ancient and rugged, a ring of mountains surrounded by the sea. It's also vital and alive, it's the last word in 'wild land' (a term used by many in the new conservationist movement) and it's Clearances Country. It was the North Lochinver estate. And now it isn't.

Like much of this quadrant of the country, Assynt has been bought and sold, regardless of the wishes of the people who lived here, over generations: traded by banks and – frequently – mountebanks; so-called property developers; collectors of faraway places; and those who just want somewhere they can blast the hell out of the local wildlife, or yank it from the river. All claimed deep financial resources, though often that amounted to little more than a long line of credit. But a few months in the late 1980s and early 1990s changed all that forever. And not just here.

At the outset, the thousands of acres around Lochinver were owned by the Vestey family, who'd made their fortune in selling meat. They decided to hive off a chunk of their land in Assynt, and created the North Lochinver Estate: 13 mostly crofting townships and a land area of over 21,000 acres. They sold it, in three separate lots, to a Swedish land speculator. It fetched over £1 million, and 'in none of these transactions', the Crofters' Trust grimly notes, 'were the interests of the people who lived and worked on the land considered to be relevant'.

Shortly afterwards came the last straw. In 1992, the new owners, Scandinavian Property Services, went bust. And, surprise, surprise, the main creditor was a

Swedish bank. The London-based liquidators put the Estate back on the market, this time in seven separate packages. The Assynt crofters had had enough.

They were increasingly angered that their land had been bought and sold from under their feet, reinforced by the fact that, as crofters, they had security of tenure. Also, they were inflamed, perhaps, by the memory of how families had been cleared in the 19th century from the glens and straths by the Duke and Duchess of Sutherland and their henchmen. So the crofters decided to launch a bid to take over the land.

They called a public meeting. They proposed – a decision judged by some people to border on the lunatic – to bid for the Estate. They set up a steering committee, made up mostly of the grazing clerks who ran agricultural affairs in the 13 townships. And the Assynt Crofters had the good fortune to have a triumvirate of ready-made leaders to hand.

Bill Ritchie, active in conservation movements and steeped in practical politics, was a ball of positive energy and someone who knew where the political levers were; John Mackenzie, a man with the air of a very shrewd bloodhound, was a patient, calm campaigner, who had retired back to his homeland and aimed to improve it; and pig breeder Alan Macrae was a diminutive firebrand, scarcely the height of one of his fence posts, but a formidable fighter in the crofting cause.

And they had a weapon available. Some years before, an unpopular law had been passed which was aimed at encouraging individual crofters to buy their own crofts. Most crofters turned their back on it, but among the powers it assigned was the right to purchase your landholding at 15 times the annual rent. Given the poor quality of the land, this was very low indeed. The crofters made sure that any potential purchaser knew that, if they did buy, half their land would be subsequently snatched away for a pittance.

So, with the support of the media, then followed by that of local public agencies, they began their campaign to raise the cash to make a bid. And they won. It took more than a year but, with the backing of government, both local and national, private individuals and the implicit support of much of the Highland media, they fought through two rejected bids to take control of the land on which they lived. This made history: and something very important had begun in the Far North.

As a journalist who covered much of the saga, what sticks in my mind is the crofters' independence: the pride and the sheer joie de vivre *of many in this Far*

North fastness. Indeed, during the period when the Swedish bank was holding out desperately against the crofters and turning down their bids, I remember plotting with a television reporter to borrow one of Alan Macrae's pigs, take it to Stockholm, and let it loose in the bank's headquarters, thereby concentrating their Scandinavian minds.

As each bid deadline passed, journalists converged on Bill Ritchie's and his family's home near the beautiful Achmelvich Beach, where he was the local ranger. Twice, we waited in vain. On one occasion I remember watching a colleague manoeuvre out of the ad hoc car park in front of the house, and reverse unerringly, for a full 400 yards, straight into the only fence post on the track. He insisted he hadn't touched a drop, but it was impressive.

The real dramming, though, took place after the crofters' final bid of around £300,000 was accepted. A ceilidh was called, fiddles were produced, and bottles rustled into view. But first came the confirmation.

Bill Ritchie brandished a book about the Highland land question and read aloud about how the local people could do nothing, as they didn't have the land. 'Well, they can rewrite their books now', he told the assembled crofters, and slammed the book down on the table in front of him: 'Because now we have the land.'

They still do. And there is life in Assynt that wasn't there before. They have developed housing, tourism, fisheries, forestry and a micro hydroelectric scheme, among others. Today, large tracts of the remotest parts of the Highlands are under community ownership. In the Western Isles, it's considerably more than half.

John Mackenzie and Bill Ritchie are still in Assynt. Allan Macrae, the conscience and the crofters' voice, is not, having died in 2013. A memorial was erected to him at Trust headquarters late in 2015. With his colleagues, he was a pioneer in a movement that is gradually reversing The Clearances.

On the Trust web site they remember him fondly. 'To us, Allan was the passion and spirit… and could always be relied on as a first line of defence for the well-being of people on the land. A light has gone out in the glen.'

Far be it for me to disagree with them, but the Assynt Crofters Estate is still casting plenty of light.

The Scottish poet Norman MacCaig loved Assynt and frequently wrote about it. He also was aware of the land tenure question. In his classic poem 'A Man in Assynt' he writes:

'Who owns this landscape?
The millionaire who bought it or
The poacher staggering downhill in the early morning
With a deer on his back?
Who possesses this landscape?
The man who bought it or
I who am possessed by it'

So it appears that the future of one of Europe's most remarkable areas will be preserved, at least for the foreseeable future. Assynt may not today be the easiest place to access, but you should make every effort to go there. You will certainly not regret your visit.

BEAULY:
LAND OF THE LOVATS

The Highlands and Islands of Scotland has over the centuries been a land of incursion, assimilation and settlement by a bewildering variety of differing peoples and cultures.

One can illustrate this process of cultural intermingling and absorption by examining the origins of some of the placenames in the Highland region. Such an analysis reveals, among others, Celtic, Pictish, Gaelic, Anglo-Saxon, Norse, Old Scots, German, Flemish, Dutch, English and, in the case of Beauly, French influences.

Beauly, an inland village of just over 1,000 inhabitants, lies 12 miles directly west of Inverness and it was, until the building of the Kessock Bridge over the Beauly Firth in 1982, located on the main A9 road leading to the Far North of Scotland.

It has been suggested that the name of the village comes from the Gaelic 'Beul Ath', meaning 'mouth of the ford', but it seems more credible that it derives from the French 'Beau Lieu' ('beautiful place') as Mary Queen of Scots described it when she stayed here in 1564, and who was clearly impressed by the place. However, the Valliscaulian monks of Burgundy, who occupied Beauly Priory from the 13th to 15th centuries, named it 'Prioritus de Bello Loco' ('priory of the lovely spot') so perhaps that's its origin. It's impossible to know with any exactitude, but today Beauly it is.

The ruins of the old Priory still exist and they are visited by thousands of people every year. King Alexander II founded the Priory, and the Cistercian Order took it over in 1510 as the Valliscaulians fell out of favour with the Pope. After the Reformation it fell into disuse and passed into the possession of the Lords of Lovat.

At the entrance to the graveyard of what must once have been a most impressive building there stands an 800-year-old elm tree, the oldest known elm tree in Europe. The Priory is currently managed and maintained by Historic Scotland, the conservationist agency of the Scottish government.

There is evidence of human habitation in the Beauly area around 2000 BC. The fertile, flat land of the Beauly Firth is ideal for settlement and agricultural use, and the village used to trade in coal, timber, fish, grain and lime. Much of the territory is the fiefdom of the Lords of Lovat, the Fraser family (whose name derives from the French word for 'strawberry', although the name 'Lovat' originates from the Gaelic for 'a dirty, smelly bog') who arrived in the wake of William the Conqueror and settled here. Other local landowners were the Chisholms and MacKenzie clans who lived north of the River Beauly, one of the finest salmon rivers in Scotland.

Beaufort Castle, three miles south of Beauly, was until recently the family seat of the Lovats. It was originally the site of a fortress, Dounie Castle, erected by the Bisset family. Then it was occupied by King Alexander I in the 12th century and besieged by Edward I, King of England, in 1303. It has been destroyed and rebuilt several times over the centuries.

The Castle was besieged and burned by Oliver Cromwell, and then again burned by the Duke of Cumberland in 1746 while Simon 'The Fox' Fraser, a leading Jacobite and the 11th Lord Lovat, was on the run after Culloden. Fraser was captured and hanged the following year in London. The present Beaufort Castle was built in the 19th century and was sold in 1994 to Ann Gloag, of the Stagecoach Group, to pay off inheritance taxes.

In the village's centre is a large square, which was originally created as a cattle market and which was laid out in its present form by the Lord Lovat of the time in the 1840s. Several chic boutiques, galleries and other such outlets line the square, and they cater to the tastes of the owners of the sought-after houses in the village's hinterland. The Lovat Arms is Beauly's largest hotel, and its distinctive red stone edifice also stands on the square.

Bourgeois Beauly

After the opening of the Kessock Bridge, Beauly could have settled into a long decline, but its changed character is mostly down to the fact that it's now on the

A862, once the busy A9, which wends gently north to Dingwall. With nothing like the same through-traffic, it's become a leafy, peaceful village, surrounded by farms: and farm shops.

These shops sell not only to tourists, but also to the many Inverness workers who have turned Beauly from a close-knit, even clannish community into a middle-class dormitory town. The agreeable café on the corner of the square doubles as a delicatessen, And Beauly also boasts a greengrocer, which is more than Inverness can offer.

This quiet little village straddles a long straight road which heads northward to Muir of Ord, the location every August of the Black Isle Show, one of Scotland's biggest agricultural events. The Glen Ord Distillery, founded in 1838 and one of the country's oldest distilleries, is still very much in operation in the town. The single malt produced here has won several international awards for its quality, and the distillery is open to visitors. From Muir of Ord you can continue north to Dingwall and the A9, west to Garve or east in the direction of Fortrose, Cromarty and the Black Isle.

Beauly is located close to Glen Affric (from the Gaelic 'Gleann Afraig': 'valley of the speckled wood'), a designated Area of Outstanding Natural Beauty and a Nature Reserve since 2001. The Glen has numerous sign-posted walks, and is populated by an array of birds and wildlife, including red, roe and Sitka deer, badgers and pine martens.

Glen Affric

Glen Affric is a gem. A short drive will take you past an art gallery in an old church and a hulking hydroelectric plant and dam. Detour just a little to the left and you come to the Falls of Plodda, five miles beyond the village of Tomich along a narrow road. After a while the tarmac stops and the road is just a forest track. Keep going and you'll reach the car park.

The Falls crash spectacularly over a drop measuring over 150 feet and create a fine mist through the forest of massive non-native Douglas firs, There's a spectacular viewing platform above the Falls, and another halfway down. The Glen is run by Forestry Commission Scotland (Coimisean na Coilltearachd Alba), and they've set up three convivial forest walks along its length. Dog Falls will take you rambling through the woods, where the Commission is gradually weeding out non-native species and re-creating the great Caledonian Pine Forest. Loch Beinn a'Mheadhain ('middle mountain') offers picnic spots and great peaceful views, but the best of all is River Affric at the head of the Glen.

You start with a steep descent from the car park, and you wander along as the river rages through rocks beside you. Then you trek up through the forest leaving the river behind as you enter a church-like silence among the firs, before looping back down to the car park. If you're reasonably fit, it's a walk of no more than half an hour. But you'll feel better for it.

Beyond the River Affric car park, the track runs out. But you can keep walking west all the way to the coast to Kintail if you have the inclination and all the right gear. It's a beautiful walk that you can do in a couple of days. There's a staffed hiker's hostel halfway there, at Altbeithe in the shadow of the Five Sisters (they're mountains), though it's not officially open in winter.

Four miles to the east of the village, just off the Inverness road, is the Moniack Castle Winery, a 16th-century tower house owned by the Fraser family, which continued the winemaking tradition established by the Priory's Burgundian monks all those centuries ago.

In recent years, Beauly railway station, which opened in 1862 and closed in 1960, was renovated and re-opened in 2002. As further evidence of the area's revitalisation, in 2010 the Scottish government approved plans to establish a new power line, with 600 pylons, from Beauly to Falkirk to carry electricity generated by wind farms elsewhere in the Highlands: a controversial decision.

Around the Beauly area there are plenty of opportunities for golf, salmon and trout fishing, walking, sailing and cycling. Beauly Shinty Club, three-times winner of the Camanachd Cup (the leading competition in Scotland) and winner of the Shinty World Cup, is also based here. The sport was brought over from Ireland by the early Irish missionaries and is claimed to have been based on Irish hurling, a sport apparently favoured by St Columba.

A word of warning: under no circumstances attempt to play shinty unless you know what you're doing. It's a rough old sport: a no-holds-barred form of hockey played by giant crofters who carry big wooden clubs, who are all determined to win and who don't like opponents getting in their way.

A bend in Beauly

*Back in the 1970s, **I** lived in a former farm cottage outside the village of Beauly. It was situated on a spectacular bend in the road to Beauly, down a track from the road. I was often woken in the night by the sound of voices where no voices should have been: somewhere in the field between our house and the road.*

On every occasion, the explanation was the same. Local residents, or indeed visitors, might have spent too convivial an evening elsewhere then had made for home and had forgotten about the bend. Thereafter, the shortest distance between two points was straight through the fence and into the field. Having established nobody was hurt (driving into a field of grain is like steering a boat into a sandbank: you generally come to a gradual stop, and there's usually nothing else to hit), I learned to retire and leave them to it. Miraculously, the car was never there in the morning.

It's always seemed to me that missing the Dumballach bend was a rite of passage for your average Beauly youth, much like running the gauntlet is to a native American, but possibly slightly less painful.

For less frantic and safer entertainment than shinty, the Beauly Pipe Band plays in the square every Thursday evening in the summer, and there is often a ceilidh of sorts to be found in one of the bars and hotels. 'Blazin' in Beauly' is a fiddle festival held every October in the village, while August offers the nearby, family-friendly annual Belladrum Tartan Heart Festival, established in 2004, which has hosted such performers as Waterboys, Seasick Steve, British Sea Power, Buzzcocks, Travis, Kaiser Chiefs and Proclaimers.

If you're heading north from Inverness, you'll find that travelling via Beauly is a gentler, more relaxed way of beginning your discovery of the Highlands than is venturing on to the busy A9. And you'll enjoy spending time in this wee place..

BONAR BRIDGE:
GATEWAY TO SUTHERLAND

There are three large estuaries on the East Highlands coastline heading north from Inverness to Wick: the Beauly, Cromarty and Dornoch Firths.

The old A9 main road to the north meandered its ponderous way around the Firths, but over the last 30 years the three Firths have been bridged. Consequently, although the road planners have revolutionised the ease and speed of access between communities of the North-East Highlands, much of interest now languishes well away from the main north-south artery and the passing motorist.

Bonar Bridge and its surrounding area is a typical example of this recent marginalisation. Before the new bridge was built across the Dornoch Firth in 1991, the main A9 road from Inverness to Wick journeyed round the southern shore of the Firth to Bonar Bridge, then a busy little place but now noticeably quieter and less hectic.

It then doubled back along the northern shore through Spinningdale and Clashmore where today it rejoins the A9. The new bridge, situated close to the mouth of the Firth, cuts out this 26-mile inland foray as it speeds the traffic along the coastal route.

Before reaching the Dornoch Firth, frequent users of the old A9 often avoided the circuitous trip round Tain by venturing over the 'Struie'. The B9176 turns inland just north of Evanton, cuts over windswept moorland and merges with what was then the main A9 road (now the A836) before reaching the village of Ardgay, many drivers having previously pulled into the layby near Easter Fearn for the spectacular 'million dollar view' over the Firth and the nearby mountains. On the following page. Iain remembers the Struie and his mis-spent youth in these parts.

Partying on the Struie

The road over the Struie, as Rab mentions, is highly recommended. Once part of the main road to and from the Far North, this is another road less travelled, through the Highlands in miniature.

For the driver, and even more the passengers, it's a delight to the eye. You rise through the green expanses of native trees, which give way to ranks of commercially planted pines. Then you ride over the cattle grid and make for the open moorland. The 'million dollar view' awaits as you begin to drop down towards the A9 again, and it can't be recommended too highly. It's a hypnotic, panoramic prospect across the Dornoch Firth delta and the hulking hills on the far side.

But there is a route which, unfortunately, cuts out this vision. You come to Aultnamain, near the top of the road, where a number of houses have been recently built. Among them is what used to be the Aultnamain Inn, where drovers once rested their cattle, and themselves, en route to selling the beasts at the mart in Dingwall.

In later years, it became a popular bar, reassuringly far from civilisation (and, in particular, its representatives who wore blue uniforms and checked caps). It was famed for the many local bands who played there: generally in a party atmosphere where clouds of indoor smoke all but camouflaged the musicians. Some of that smoke came from cigarettes. Understandably, everyone enjoyed the music.

Today, the Aultnamain Inn is gone, but just beyond it you can turn right down a narrow road, with passing places, to the village of Edderton. It too has its attractions, which used to include a shop selling corn dollies, if you like that sort of thing.

Ardgay is a pleasant wee place, and was home to the justifiably renowned Lady Ross Tearooms (which once boasted a splendid jukebox containing music ranging from Jimmy Shand to The Mothers of Invention), and is located at the entrance to Strathcarron. The village's railway station, which used to be called Bonar Bridge station, is on the Far North Line which carries the traveller from the teeming city of Inverness to the austere but eerily beautiful county of Caithness.

A mile or so north along the road from Ardgay sits Bonar Bridge, at one time the gateway to the county of Sutherland. Bonar Bridge is on the north bank of the Kyle of Sutherland, which is fed upstream by the rivers Oykel, Cassley, Shin and Carron and which, in turn, develops into the wide Dornoch Firth. Many of the placenames in and around the town are of Norse origin, as the Firth was the boundary between the old provinces of Cat (originally Pictish, then Norse) and Ross. Its prehistory is indicated by the presence of hut circle and cairn remains. Also, in 1900 a hoard of Bronze Age jewellery, dating to 2000 BC, was discovered at Tulloch Hill behind Bonar. Known as 'The Migdale Hoard', this collection currently resides in The National Museum of Scotland in Edinburgh.

In the 14th century Bonar was the location of an iron foundry, with the iron ore coming from the west, and salmon fishing was also economically important to the settlement. During The Wars of The Three Kingdoms, Carbisdale, three miles to the north of Bonar, was the scene of a battle in 1650 between the Royalists, under the Marquis of Montrose, and the Scottish Covenanter government, who emerged victorious. Montrose fled the battle, was captured, and taken to Edinburgh where he was hanged.

Bonar was an old ferrying point over the Kyle and was often used by cattle drovers heading south (the town's name 'Bonar' derives from the Gaelic 'Am Ban Ath': 'the fair ford'). In 1809 an overladen ferry boat sank at the Meikle Ferry near the mouth of the Firth and 99 passengers, including the Sheriff of Dornoch, were drowned. Something had to be done so, in 1812, a Telford-designed cast-iron bridge was opened, and Bonar became Bonar Bridge. The bridge stood for 80 years but was swept away by a flood (an event apparently predicted by the Brahan Seer, the 17th-century Highland visionary).

A steel-and-granite second bridge was erected in 1893, and today's bridge was built in 1973. Having crossed this arched bridge from Ardgay into Bonar, as a driver you have few options other than to turn left and westward towards Lairg and Loch Shin or take a right to go east along the Firth and to the A9.

There are several intriguing places of historical interest in the Bonar area, one being Carbisdale Castle across the Kyle of Sutherland. It was built between 1905 and 1917 for the Duchess of Sutherland, wife of the third Duke and a lady who was unpopular with the Sutherland family. Although she was the beneficiary of the Duke's will ('all my worldly goods'), on his death in 1892 the family contested this, and the Duchess ended up spending six weeks in prison in London for forging documentation. Eventually, the family agreed to provide her with a financial settlement and also to build her a castle, on the condition that it must not be on Sutherland lands. The Duchess, however, was nursing a grievance.

She built Carbisdale Castle in Ross-shire, on a hill facing Sutherland, and this 'folly' was unmissable from the main road and rail links to and from the county. The clock on the tower faces in only three directions, the one opposite Invershin in Sutherland being blank, so she didn't have to give her former relatives the time of day. It is no surprise, then, that it is known as 'Castle Spite'. It was used as the residence for the King of Norway during World War II and given thereafter to the Scottish Youth Hostel Association. It was closed for repairs in 2011 and is currently up for sale, as Iain explains.

A ghost called Betty

Carbisdale Castle may still be a handsome hulk in search of a future… but it may just have had a narrow escape. The owners, the Scottish Youth Hostel Association, thought they'd sold it off to developers Aberdeen Capital Ltd., who promised '21 spellbinding suites' and 90 jobs in a five-star hotel. The SYHA stripped the place out, flogging off a huge art collection that used to decorate the Castle walls – yes, even when it was a youth hostel – in May 2015 at Sotheby's, raising over a million quid. Seventeen sculptures and 36 Italian and Scottish 19th-century paintings went under the hammer.

But then doubts arose about the sale and, in April 2016, SYHA announced they were calling it off, saying it was 'as a result of growing concerns as to the likelihood of the sale ultimately being achieved'. The company hit back, suggesting they'd just found out the local community wanted to buy woodland around the castle and a wind farm was proposed for nearby. It's fair to say there are doubts about these excuses locally – but a lot of relief, too.

The SYHA says it still intends to sell – though it's not clear whether they'll be mentioning Aberdeen Capital again – or indeed the fact that the castle has a resident ghost. She is, apparently, called Betty. A spokesperson for Betty declined to claim credit for the collapse of the sale. Meanwhile, what will happen to the mountain-biking trails and the popular and well-laid-out walks in and around the Castle grounds? This remains to be seen. Maybe you should try them before they disappear?

A few miles to the west of Ardgay, along an old track, sits Croick Old Parish Church, where occurred a major event in the history of The Clearances. Iain relates the story.

'the wicked generation'

During the 19th-century Highland Clearances, James Gillanders, factor for the Robertsons of Kindeace, succeeded in 1845 in moving 18 families (around 90 people) from Glencalvie, a few miles to the west of Bonar.

Many of them took shelter in nearby Croick churchyard in makeshift bothies, and the inscriptions on the windows – such as a line reading 'Glencalvie Folk: the wicked generation' – document how they were persuaded by their minister that it was somehow their fault, and was due punishment for their sins. In this, the clergy of the time, beholden for their very living in many cases to the lairds who were doing the clearance, have an inglorious history.

Someone else about whom that can be said was the woman who wrote the slavery saga Uncle Tom's Cabin: *Harriet Beecher Stowe, an anti-slavery campaigner. In her book* Sunny Memories of Foreign Lands, *she supported The Clearances, and particularly her friends the Duke and Duchess of Sutherland, saying they had elevated 'in a few years… the whole community to a point of education and material prosperity which unassisted (it) might never have attained'.*

That triggered an angry response from exiled Sutherland man Donald Macleod in one of the most famous accounts of The Clearances, which he entitled Gloomy Memories… *and, Ms Stowe and the Sutherlands aside, he had this to say about the clergy: 'the foulest deeds were glossed over and all the evil which could be attributed to the natives themselves… was by these pious gentlemen ascribed to providence, as a punishment for sin'.*

Suffice to say that many of his fellow Highlanders took a similarly jaundiced view, and many were to flock to the ranks of the Free Church of Scotland, which, however it is regarded by non-believers these days, back then pulled no forelock to the lairds and opposed clearings at every turn. It's worth pointing out that all but two families who attended Croick Church followed their minister into the Free Church in 1843.

The little church at Croick, meanwhile, looks much as it did, inside and out. The interior is all dark pews and filtered light, with the London Times *account of The Clearances and an explanation of the inscriptions given due prominence in a small display. The inscriptions themselves can still be read in the window glass. Among them is another, documenting another clearing, at Greenyards in Strathcarron in March 1854, which came to be known as 'The Massacre of the Rosses'.*

One final irony. Late last century the Croick Estate was acquired by a company who were hell-bent on running it as a sporting estate for those who wished to shoot deer and to fish for salmon. To this end, they set about evicting the tenant of the Estate's massive sheep farm. And a public campaign arose to stop them. Today, under new ownership, the sheep, in whose name The Clearances took place, have been mostly phased out and the Estate now markets itself as a walker-friendly, tourist attraction.

But the Glencalvie folk are gone.

As well as being of major historical importance, the area contains many natural attractions for the visitor to the area. Pehaps the best known is the Falls of Shin on the River Shin to the north of Bonar in the direction of Lairg.

Lairg in unique in the Highlands, in that, with its population of around 1,000, it is the only settlement of any size which is not coastal. Indeed, it sits in the centre of the North Highlands, nestling sedately at the southern end of the 17-mile-long Loch Shin, and is known as the 'Crossroads of Sutherland'. Its position, and the fact that it is on the Far North Line, makes it an ideal spot for tourists to use as a base for travelling to the north and the west.

At the Falls of Shin between May and November, and especially during the late summer months, Atlantic salmon return upstream through the Dornoch Firth to their spawning grounds to breed. Although the Falls are not very high, the flow of water is powerful, and the magnificent sight of the salmon leaping up the downwardly rushing torrent in their attempt to return home well illustrates the persistence of the world of nature and the determination of these splendid silver fish.

In 2002 Harrods' owner Mohamed-Al-Fayed established The Falls of Shin Visitor Centre, which contained a restaurant, a branch of Harrods department store (in the middle of Sutherland?) and a waxwork model of himself to remind everyone who's boss. He sold Harrods in 2010 but retained the Centre, which severed its connection with Harrods. 'The Harrods of the North' was destroyed by fire in May 2013. While a shop is operating here at present, planning permission has recently been granted for the development of a new Centre.

On the slopes to the east of the Kyle and north of Bonar stretches Balblair Forest, a Forestry Commission-owned extensive woodland with waymarked paths and tracks for walkers, cyclists and those on horseback. Also, the fishing opportunities around Bonar are plentiful, with brown trout at Loch Buidhe and salmon and sea trout in the Kyle of Sutherland, and the River Oykel is one of Scotland's finest salmon rivers. There is a nine-hole moorland golf course to the north of Bonar if you are in need of a rest from this glorious natural backdrop.

So there is plenty to do, observe and contemplate if you turn off the A9 just after Tain and head inland. It's well worth the diversion.

BRORA:

INDUSTRY, WILDLIFE AND BEACHES

Over the centuries, the inhabitants of the Highlands generally have been dependent for their livelihoods largely on fishing, service industries and farming of various sorts: subsistence activities rather than the manufacturing of goods and products for wider markets.

There have been a few attempts at making stuff but, by and large, this was not a talent that most Highlanders possessed or wished to develop. This is not to imply laziness: quite the opposite, in fact, as their daily existence depended on arduous physical labour. Rather, it was indicative of a general desire for a quiet and peaceful life, with enough to eat, somewhere comfortable to sleep and a few well-deserved drams at the end of the day, and there's nothing wrong with that.

Industrial development in the Highlands on any meaningful scale was a post-World War II phenomenon, which included, among other ventures, the generation of hydroelectric power, the aluminium smelter at Invergordon, and particularly the discovery and exploitation of North Sea oil. So it's rare indeed to come across a Highland area with an industrial heritage dating back to the early 16th century.

This exception to the general rule is Brora, a coastal town of around 1,000 inhabitants in East Sutherland. Today, it's popular with tourists: its long, sandy beach, the surrounding wildlife and countryside and its renowned golf course proving irresistible to many visitors. I've driven through Brora on numerous ooccasions, stopped off for a pint and maybe a game of golf, and then continued along the A9, unaware of the town's unique historical status. However, I recently discovered a few intriguing facts about the place.

What I hadn't known (and I should have done) was that, unlike its coastal neighbours of Dornoch, Golspie and Helmsdale, almost 500 years ago Brora had taken its first steps to becoming a significant manufacturing and industrial centre. Open-cast coal mining began close to the sea as early as 1529, the oldest such excavation in Europe, and the first pit shaft was sunk further inland in 1598, with a couple of deeper shafts sunk later as demand grew.

The coal was used by the local salt industry, with the first saltpans also opening in 1598. Although the economic fortunes of Brora's coal and salt industries fluctuated over the years, by the early 19th century Brora was exporting 400 tons of salt from its tiny harbour, one of the smallest in Britain. That's a lot of salt.

This little town has also enthusiastically embraced fish curing, shipbuilding, wool and textile industries, lemonade manufacture, a distillery and a brickworks. Jurassic sandstone extracted from its stone quarry was used in the construction of London Bridge. The brickworks was in place in 1818, the Clynelish Distillery was established in 1819 and a new harbour had been completed by 1830.

Stafford Arms

Brora is one of the few parts of the Northern Highlands that benefited from the actions of the First Duke and Duchess of Sutherland, formerly the Marquis of Stafford and Lady Stafford. Her Ladyship was responsible for setting up a brewery, the Stafford Arms, by the harbour, in 1817. Himself was behind the creation of the original Clynelish Distillery a year later, and in 1821 he commissioned the building of a new harbour. According to the local website, it became a centre for import and export and 'even a starting place for emigrants to New Zealand'. Imagine...

In 1901 a wool mill was established, and in 1913 the village was the first place in the Northern Highlands to have its own electricity supply, which was required for the wool mill and was also used for street lighting. The locals named the place 'Electric City'. Mains electricity did not arrive in the Sutherland area until after World War II, so Brora was also a pioneer in energy production.

The name of the town in Gaelic is 'Brura' which in turn derives from the Old Norse 'Brua-a', meaning 'river with a bridge', the river being the River Brora: today's bridge spans the gorge in the centre of the town. Standing stones, brochs, chambered cairns and hill forts are to be found in abundance around Brora, indicating a sizeable prehistoric and Pictish presence in the area. Originally called Inverbrora, the village was chartered as a Burgh in 1345.

In the early 19th century many victims of The Clearances, particularly virulent in Sutherland, settled here. So, by the early 20th century, it was a populous, thriving and hard-working community. As the century progressed, however, competition from the south and elsewhere gradually eroded Brora's industrial base. By the mid-1970s the brickworks had finally closed down and the coal mine been demolished and filled in. The closure of the wool mill in 2002 effectively marked the end of the town as an industrial area, although a distillery is still in production and is particularly cherished for its 15-year-old Clynelish single malt.

However, the industrial impetus continues offshore. Around 15 miles east off the coast from Brora in the North Sea is the Beatrice Oil Field, a small field with declining capacity. In 2007 two deep-water wind turbines were erected near to the field with the generated electricity going to a nearby rig. The turbine owners hope and expect that the turbines will supply enough power to compensate for the energy currently provided by the oil field once the oil dries up: an interesting experiment in 'clean' technology, and one increasingly being emulated across the Highlands.

Brora is also popular with sport fans, particularly followers of golf and football (*for the latter, see Iain's 'The Wee Rangers' article below*), both very much Scottish games despite some impertinent protestations to the contrary. Brora's golf course was re-modelled by James Baird in 1932 and was described by Open ex-champion Peter Thomson as 'the best traditional links course in the world'.

When I played it, I found the electricified wires around the greens somewhat disconcerting,. It was explained to me that cows and sheep are allowed to roam the course, under ancient grazing rights, and the wire keeps them off the more sensitive areas. Cowpats, incidentally, are regarded as 'casual water' so you get a free drop. Because of the animals' grazing, the rough is forgiving, although it's a hilly, challenging course but not too difficult for a decent golfer.

The Wee Rangers

Brora Rangers are the 'wee Rangers', but in recent seasons they've been very 'big' Rangers, at least in the Highland League. Mind you, they've had to wait a bit for glory. Founded in 1879, they'd never won the League title till 2013-14. A link-up with Premier League Ross County has done no harm at all, and the club set several post-War records in that title-winning season.

They're the most northerly club to have won the title. They also had the most points ever collected, the greatest margin of victory (20 points), the highest number of wins (31 out of 34), the highest goal difference (plus 107), and conceded the fewest goals (16). They went on to win their way through the first half of the following season, so that, in the calendar year 2014, they were unbeaten, and had extended that run to 57 matches across three seasons until they finally lost a match in August 2015.

By then, they'd already again won the title, having gone the entire 2014-15 season unbeaten and having broken the record for goals scored in a single season. All of this success meant they had to go into promotion playoffs, under the latest Scottish League reorganisation, which had introduced a pyramid structure, taking in the Highland and Lowland Leagues. Brora beat Edinburgh City, from the Lowlands, on penalties and were then pitched into a match with the bottom-placed club in League Two, Montrose, for a place in the Scottish League.

Brora's supporters and club bosses had so far thoroughly enjoyed the glory. But the prospect of having to travel all over Scotland to play at grounds more run-down, and more poorly attended, than their own Dudgeon Park, did not entice. The fans wanted a vote but were denied, and their chairman – in what was not the most stirring of battle cries – confirmed 'there's no way we can avoid competing... we can't opt out, we've got to go for it'.

And so they did, sort of. Brora won the first leg 1-0 at home. But in the away leg they lost 3-1 and Montrose kept their place. It has not been officially confirmed that there was dancing in the streets of Brora but strangely, in the following Highland League season, they were no longer at the head of the pack for much of the campaign.

Wildlife abounds in the Brora area. There are facilities for horse riding, pony trekking, angling, deer stalking and mountain biking, among other healthy pursuits. The River Brora is one of the most under-rated angling rivers in Britain, and its dark pools and fast-flowing, clean water is famed for its salmon and trout.

Arctic terns (known locally as 'sea swallows' and which are the emblem of the Golf Club) spend their summers on the beach, and fly over the sea alongside curlews, oyster catchers, buzzards and the occasional golden eagle. The high waves are ideal for surfing and you can watch seals from the harbour's edge.

As for local entertainment, there are a few bars and restaurants, and at the end of July there's the Brora Carnival Week. And you shouldn't miss out on

Capaldi's, the town's old ice cream parlour. It doesn't sound like a particularly lively cultural scene, but I guess most people don't visit Brora for the rock 'n roll. Just ask around and you'll find out what's happening. But make sure you don't fall foul of some of the local judiciary, as Iain here narrates.

A most peculiar Sheriff

Despite its charms, Brora has not always appealed to everyone. Indeed, one prominent critic, Sheriff Ewan Stewart, sat over a number of years on the judicial bench. He once described Brora as 'a hotbed of crime' and its youth as 'rotten, loud-mouthed drunks'. And he told one accused he was astonished that he'd lived into his twenties in Brora, and yet never appeared before the bench.

Mind you, Sheriff Stewart was not your average judge. In 1992, he was finally removed from his position by the then-Secretary of State for Scotland after a BBC Scotland sting recorded him voicing some very unwise opinions about his fellow Sheriffs and other prominent members of the legal profession in Scotland: though obviously that wasn't the reason he was sacked. Dear me, no.

In his time, the good Sheriff was known to fall asleep during trials, or have lunch in a hotel next to the court with the accused who had been standing in the dock before him that morning. In Dingwall, he asked a farmer if he had names for each of his flock, explaining his first law of sheep: 'Like Chinamen they all look the same but they have different personalities'.

A number of his findings were thrown out on appeal, with one senior judge saying they'd had to warn him several times 'that he must not take into account irrelevant material, sheer speculation, nor material discovered by his own researches or which proceeds on local gossip'.

After his sacking, he decided in 1999 to run for Parliament. He wanted to have trawlers electronically tagged, and for the Queen to pass the Crown Estate over to the Prince of Wales. And he appealed to farmers not to commit suicide: going bankrupt was not a disgrace, he said, and he would call round with advice.

Not that he called round at the doors of many voters during an election. He found a Betterware brush salesman, who volunteered to deliver his election leaflets for him. He lost, and in 2000 he passed away in his home in Wick. So you can't visit him, which should be a matter for some regret. Though possibly not in Brora.

Brora is only one hour's drive from Inverness and is also on the Far North Line, so it's easy enough to access. It's as relaxing a place as any to discover the coastal pleasures of East Sutherland, of which there are many.

CROMARTY:

DOLPHINS, OIL AND THE BLACK ISLE

Recently I was chatting with an old mate of mine, and our conversation turned to the small seaport of Cromarty, a few miles north of Inverness on the Black Isle (which is not, in fact, an 'Isle' but a peninsula, known in Gaelic as 'an t-Eilean Dubh'). He reminded me of an incident from my self-indulgent youth.

I was a 'roadie' at a venue in Cromarty with his dance band in which he was playing guitar. I have no recollection of this, having probably overdone the Glenmorangie, but apparently I jumped on the stage, shoved aside the organist and started to play the instrument under the belief that I was Jerry Lee Lewis. I had never played keyboards before in my life, and I gather that this became quickly apparent. The band was furious, the audience noisily and increasingly expressed their displeasure, and my mate speedily 'escorted' me from the venue.

I have always liked Cromarty but, since then, I've been a bit apprehensive about walking around the town in case I bump into one of the audience, who may have a long memory. They're hard men in Cromarty. But Iain (*below*) reassures me.

That's a relief

My esteemed co-author, in his above reminiscences of the Cromarty of his youth, expresses his concern about the village's hard men having long memories. He need no longer be concerned.

These days, Cromarty is a douce dormitory town, with its own artistic-minded middle class, who would be more inclined to drink you to death with a nice Chablis than indulge in unseemly violence with the empty bottle. The town's bourgeois status was recently confirmed when the Prince of Wales described it as 'a jewel in the crown of vernacular architecture'.

Today a town of fewer than 1,000 inhabitants, Cromarty sits at the tip of the Cromarty Firth betwen the Sutors, high rocks on the north and south entrances to the Firth. 'Sutor' is Old Scots for 'shoemaker', and the rocks contain the remains of once substantial gun emplacements designed to protect the Firth. They were established in the early 20th century and abandoned in the 1950s.

Cromarty's etymology is somewhat confusing. The 'crom' bit is Gaelic for 'crooked', while the 'arty' comes either from the Gaelic words 'bati' (bay) or 'ard' (height). So let's call it 'the bend between the heights'. It becomes more complicated when one discovers that its Gaelic name is today 'Cromba' while, as a mediaeval town in the late 12th century, it was known as 'Crumbathyn' and was a Royal Burgh and home to the Earls of Cromartie.

The town grew around the harbour, and it was a herring centre and ferry port for centuries. There is evidence that King James IV, in the 15th century, as well as other Scottish monarchs, passed through Cromarty via the Kessock Ferry at Inverness, and then onward to Tain to pay homage to St Duthac's shrine. Their means of passage was known as the 'Kings' Route'.

By the 1700s Cromarty was a thriving Burgh, exporting salt fish and the local hemp fibre. It also had fish-processing works, shipbuilding facilities, and agricultural improvements were continually being made to the surrounding parishes. However, The Clearances continued across the area.

For instance, in 1838, 280 local people set sail from Cromarty to America in a less than seaworthy vessel, and records reveal a good deal of conflict across the Black Isle between the dispossessed crofters and the new sheep farmers and local landlords.

Nevertheless, during the 19th century the town seemed as if it might equal Inverness as a major Highland trading port. However, in the early 20th century an economic decline was becoming apparent in Cromarty. The herring stocks were diminishing in the North Sea and, although work started in 1902 on a railway link to the Inverness-Dingwall line, it was abandoned in 1914 as World War I began.

Death in the Firth

One of Britain's biggest naval disasters took place just off Cromarty, a British naval base during World War I, when HMS Natal blew up and sank there in December 1915. Captain Eric Black was hosting a film party aboard and had invited some local worthies – and some nearby nurses.

Just before half past three in the afternoon, a series of explosions tore through the rear of the ship, sinking it in minutes. Over 400 died. It was originally thought she'd been torpedoed by a U-Boat or hit by a mine, but divers concluded that it was probably an explosion in an ammunition magazine that started the disaster.

After the explosion, her hull was still visible at low water, and Royal Navy vessels entering and leaving the Firth would sound 'still', bringing officers and men to attention. Though some of the ship was salvaged over the years, the final indignity came in the 1970s when it was blown up again, to prevent it becoming a hazard to navigation.

During this economic downturn, there was also an agricultural crisis affecting much of the Highlands, and emigration was once again seen as the answer, so much so that the population of Cromarty declined from 2,000 in 1914 to 837 in 1931. However, as the Scottish economy generally improved, so did that of Cromarty, aided by an increase in tourism and further improvements in agriculture, but particularly by the arrival of the North Sea oil boom in the early 1970s. US oil company Brown & Root selected Nigg Bay, across the Firth from Cromarty, as the site for an oilrig fabrication yard, and soon giant cranes and platforms were dwarfing the local scenery.

This sudden intrusion of these massive man-made superstructures, however, appears to have had little impact on the local sea life, on which much of the local economy depends. Between Cromarty and, in particular around Chanonry Point on Rosemarkie Bay a few miles to the south on the Moray Firth, live schools of bottlenose dolphins. The area is regarded as the best place in Europe to see these magnificent mammals, soaring elegantly from the sea.

The town, relatively small though it may be, is of serious architectural importance: there are carefully preserved 18th-century Georgian houses; the Courthouse, a Grade A listed building built in 1733, houses the Museum; the 'Old Church' is one of the best-preserved Presbyterian churches in Scotland;

Cromarty House is on the site of the old castle of the Earls of Ross; the 'Old Orchard' is a reconstructed garden surrounding Cromarty's oldest inhabited house (c 1690); and the thatched-roof birthplace of Hugh Miller, born in 1801 and a stonemason, geologist, author and Cromarty's most celebrated citizen, still stands near his statue on Church Street.

It was Miller whose research suggested that an older Cromarty had been submerged under the North Sea by rising sea levels, a problem the town continues to face. An archaeological dig is currently under way close to the beach to the east of Cromarty, as exposed foundations of old buildings have recently been discovered there. It is conceivable that Miller's theory could well be proved correct, and that Cromarty is a more ancient settlement than has till now been assumed.

Artistically and culturally, Cromarty is a vibrant little community. Every New Year's Day the town hosts the popoular annual 'Splash and Dash', a free community enterprise which involves a dip in the Dornoch Firth (do you have any idea how cold that would be?) followed by a 3km or 6km run, and it is always a well-attended event.

The town's best known artistic happening, however, is the annual Film Festival, which has been held over a weekend every December since 2007.

Film Festival

The Cromarty Film Festival, which bears the label of 'My Favourite Festival', features great films and the opportunity for celeb spotting.

The Festival invites various weel-kent characters to pick their five favourite films, come along to a screening of one of them, and talk to the audience about why they like it. Over the years, those guests have included singer Eddi Reader, painter and writer John Byrne, Inverness-born author Ali Smith, movie maestro Michael Caton Jones, Kirsty Wark off the telly, writer A L Kennedy, funny man Sanjeev Kholi, Deacon Blue's Ricky Ross and Lorraine McIntosh, the late Tony Benn, writer Ian Rankin, actor David Hayman, Dr Who director Douglas Mackinnon, director Bill Forsyth and, er, me. (It was Pan's Labyrinth, since you ask.)

I should say that my fellow scribbler has never received an invite: clearly, he's not of sufficient intellectual calibre (the 'fellow scribbler' writes: 'I had to spell

'Labyrinth' for him, though'). *The point is not to burnish my own ego (though obviously that's important) but to illustrate there are things going on in Cromarty that you might not expect to find out on the tip of the Black Isle.*

The Festival can end up showing films just about anywhere: on lighthouses, gable ends, ships' sails or on a big screen. It doesn't matter. As one critic put it, comparing the weekend event to places like Cannes and Toronto: 'Cromarty Film Festival includes the one thing usually missing from the festival big boys: fun. It can screen Airplane, This Is Spinal Tap *and* Duck Soup *without qualms.' Admittedly that review appeared on the Festival's own website, but the reviewer involved isn't part of the team and genuinely goes back every year. And I agree with her, for what that's worth.*

Incidentally, the abovementioned Ian Rankin, author of the 'Rebus' crime novels, maintains a Highland hideaway in Cromarty. In the novel Standing In Another Man's Grave *he finally coaxed his curmudgeonly detective away from Edinburgh and drew him up the A9 by way of a series of murders to his home-away-from-home.*

Cromarty was the place where Rankin returned to writing after the early death of his contemporary Iain Banks, and the urgings of his wife had persuaded him to abandon the laptop and live a little. He told a book festival audience how he sat down in his house in Cromarty, where he has no wi-fi and no TV, to write his latest Rebus, Even Dogs In The Wild.

'I took my old coal-fired laptop up there and did 100 pages of the book in 10 days, 30,000 words', he said. 'It just flew. I couldn't believe it. It was like everything was just sitting there waiting.'

Also, Cromarty has added to its artistic allure with the establishment of the Arts Trust, which encourages and fosters local activities from ukulele playing (a more difficult instrument than you may think) via stonemasonry to stained glass design. There are also the Fiddle Weekend, the Harp Village Festival and assorted other musical events held in local bars and hotels. I'm not sure if the music venue where I unwisely performed my Jerry Lee Lewis impersonation still exists. Perhaps it would be wise not to ask.

Anyway, you're bound to find something in Cromarty that suits your taste. Just make sure you can play the piano properly if you're going out for a few drinks in the evenings.

CULLODEN:
STRATHNAIRN, CLAVA CAIRNS
AND DRUMOSSIE MOOR

As you leave Inverness heading south on the A9, the first stretch leads you through some flat moorland until, having travelled six miles or so, the road bends down to the right, and then up again. This is the hamlet of Daviot, and from then on the scenery becomes hillier and more rugged as you head up to Carrbridge, Aviemore and the Grampian Mountains.

The River Nairn travels through Daviot (from the Pictish 'Deimidh' meaning 'strong place') and the River then meanders past such historic places as Culloden Forest, the ancient Clava Cairns, the magnificent Culloden Viaduct and the infamous Culloden Battlefield, until it enters the Moray Firth at Nairn, 15 miles to the east of Inverness.

Daviot Church was granted its charter in the 13th century, and survived the turmoils of the Reformation and the 'Disruption' of 1843, when the Free Church split from the Church of Scotland. It used to be known as 'the kirk of the golden cockerel' due to its distinctive weather vane. The existing building was completely restored in 1991. The father of Alistair MacLean, the thriller writer, is buried in the churchyard, and MacLean, whose first language was Gaelic, was brought up in Daviot.

 Daviot House, another building of some repute, was built in the 1820s by the 24th Chief of the Clan MacKintosh, a family which has lived in the Inverness area for a while. Indeed, the first Chief of the Clan MacKintosh was appointed Keeper of Inverness Castle in 1179, so they must have seen a few changes over the years.

Although Daviot Forest is a sheltered spot, and there is a well-laid-out walk through the woods, the nearby Drumossie Moor can be a cold, windy and wild place in winter. However, not everyone finds this to be the case. One evening at closing time at our Inverness drinking den, a 70-year-old friend of mine decided to walk to his Daviot home although there was a fierce snowstorm raging.

He reached Drumossie Moor and, feeling the effects of his earlier drams, decided to have a sleep beside the path. When he woke up some hours later he was covered by at least a couple of feet of snow. He stood up, brushed the snow off his thin raincoat, resumed his journey home and ate a hearty breakfast, none the worse for what would have been, for an average human being, a near-death experience. They breed them tough in the Hielans.

As one heads directly north from Daviot in the direction of Culloden along the B9006, it is almost impossible, and highly inadvisable, to miss the Culloden Viaduct, which carries Highland Main Line trains over the River Nairn and into Inverness station. This red stone architectural masterpiece, designed by Murdoch Paterson who was Chief Engineer to the Highland Railway, is an object of awe and wonder. It was built in 1898, has 28 spans and is 1800 feet in length, making it the largest masonry viaduct in Scotland. It is a Category A listed building, and more than deserves its exalted status.

Close to the Viaduct, and only a few hundred yards away from Culloden Battlefield, is one of Scotland's archaeological treasures: the Clava Cairns. This site, just off the road, consists of three well-preserved Bronze Age chamber tomb cairns, enclosed by stone circles. These magnificent examples of chamber tombs date back at least 4,000 years, and their precise and formal layout suggests that the builders were sun worshippers.

The striking Culloden Forest is also nearby. It is mainly planted with conifers, such as Scots pine, Norway and Sitka spruce and Douglas fir, as well as beech, alder and birch trees. In the Forest you will find St Mary's Well (or, as it was originally called, the 'clootie well'), which in Celtic times was a Druidic shrine where locals would hang cloths ('cloots') in order to ward off evil spirits.

The Forest was first owned by the MacKintoshes, who also built the original Culloden House in 1626, but the Forbes family took over the running of the Forest and rebuilt the House in a palatial, Classical style in 1783 after the original building was destroyed by fire. The Forbes family lived there until 1897, and the Forestry Commission assumed management of the Forest in 1926.

The Battle of Culloden, fought in April 1746 between Jacobite followers of the

Stuarts and the Duke of Cumberland's Hanoverian Army, was the last battle fought on British soil. It has been the subject of innumerable books and films, so we will not dwell overlong on it here. Suffice to say that it was a triumph for the Hanoverians and the Highland clans who fought alongside them, and that the tactics and discipline of the British Army resulted in the massacre of the Jacobites, despite the bravery of many Highlanders whose typical charge, claymores in hand, proved ultimately disastrous.

The Battle of Culloden

The site of the last battle fought on the British mainland – on 16 April 1746 – is Drumossie Moor, some four miles to the south-east of the city centre of Inverness.

To get there, follow the B9006 road, and you will find an impressive Visitors' Centre with considerable car parking all around. Or you can walk out onto the battlefield itself, if you prefer not to pay for the many attractions of the Centre, which was built at a cost of around £9.5 million and was opened in 2007.

There is much to admire in the Centre: weapons that were used in the battle; a mind-blowing battle room, in which you can stand and be fired on by both sides; a large animated battle table, showing you what happened and where; and, as well as the inevitable restaurant and shop, you can go out on top of the building to work out the tactics and co-ordinates used during the battle.

The myth is that the Highland Jacobite army, heroically led by the fabled Bonnie Prince Charlie, was gallantly defeated by the cruel Hanoverians led by the Duke of Cumberland. Well, yes and no. Here are a few facts to go along with some of the fallacies which you may have been told.

• There were as many, if not more, Highlanders fighting for the government forces as fought for the Jacobites, and a number of clans decided to take no part in Charlie's attempted coup.

• The 1745/46 Rebellion was not a war of independence: rather it was a civil war between two dynastic monarchies, which led to the end of the Stuart challenge for the Scottish crown.

• The night before the battle, the Jacobites marched to Nairn, where the government troops were getting tanked up to celebrate the 25th birthday of their commander,

the Duke of Cumberland. But the Jacobites got lost and decided to turn back to Culloden as the day began to dawn. Many of the Highlanders, therefore, hadn't slept or eaten, when battle was subsequently joined.

• It was scarcely a battle at all, lasting under an hour and ending with an estimated 1250 Jacobite dead, with only 50 government troops killed.

• Most of the Highlanders were cut down by artillery and musket fire before they even reached the government lines.

• The battlefield, today restored to something like the bare, boggy moorland it actually was in 1746, was exactly the wrong sort of ground for the Highlanders, famous for their berserker charges, to fight on. Guess who chose it?

• Bonnie Prince Charlie was a crap commander. On the eve of the battle he had fired his highly successful general Lord George Murray – reputed never to have lost in combat – and had himself taken charge, with the help of an Irish adjutant who was, frankly, an idiot.

• He placed the Macdonalds – yes, that would be my mob – on the left flank, when they were accustomed to fighting in a place of honour on the right. They are said to have refused to take part, though they were in amongst the soggiest ground, and may not have had much opportunity, before being overrun.

• As Charlie's army was cut to pieces, he panicked and ran away. Or as a song has it, 'he ran like a rabbit down the glen'.

He eventually escaped back to France, having been sheltered by courageous Highlanders for several months, despite a considerable price (thirty thousand pounds, which was a fortune in those days) on his head. According to some sources, he actually returned to the UK, to London, in 1750, where he lived for a time. He had two wives, both of whom he beat so badly that they ran away and left him. After a thoroughly debauched and drunken life, he died an alcoholic wreck in Rome.

The price of Charlie's little adventure was social repression verging on racial cleansing in the Highlands, the destruction of the clan system and, eventually, the Highland Clearances.

Way to go, Charlie.

Such was the nature of Cumberland's vicious cruelty to innocent people on his troops' march back to Inverness after the battle that he acquired the nickname 'Butcher' Cumberland. The Hanoverians took many highly ranked Jacobite prisoners. Many of those who were not immediately shot were executed in Inverness or were taken down to London and publicly hanged.

The events at Culloden gave the British government the excuse they needed to bring the Highlands under central control and to extinguish the possibility of further rebellions emanating from the North of Scotland. The government banned the Gaelic language and Highland dress, and suppressed the people, often savagely. The government's attitude changed when they discovered the quality and bravery of the Highlanders as British Army troops. Indeed, only a few years after Culloden, many exiled Highlanders fought on the government side in the American Wars of Independence, and later served under Wellington in his Napoleonic campaigns.

By the early 19th century, the myth of romantic 'Highlandism', and all the rewriting of history which this required, was born, and we have had to learn to live with it ever since. As so often in Scottish history, legend and myth obscure the truth.

Today, however, on the drive down from the battlefield and Drumossie to Inverness, one cannot fail to be impressed by the wonderful panoramic view across the Beauly Firth to the Black Isle and beyond, with the Kessock Bridge as the elegant centrepiece and Ben Wyvis as the backdrop.

The city of Inverness, home to around 80,000 people, may not be the most beautiful settlement in the Highlands but its surrounding landscape more than compensates. The Strathnairn area is a fine example of what can be found around the city, and it is a fascinating day trip from Inverness.

DINGWALL:
PROSPEROUS COUNTY TOWN

The bustling town of Dingwall, with its population of just under 6,000, sits at the head of the Cromarty Firth and has long been the market town and administrative centre of the Easter Ross area. It was at one time a small port, built by Thomas Telford in the 1820s, but gradual silting up of the Firth means it is now an inland settlement. Today there remains little obvious evidence of its coastal past.

Although in Gaelic it is known as 'Inbhir Pheofharain' ('mouth of the River Peffer'), its modern name 'Dingwall' derives from the Old Norse 'Bingvolir', meaning a 'meeting place' or 'local assembly'. A Norse settlement from the late 9th century, it became of strategic importance as it was located close to where the Norse lands met the Kingdom of the Scots and, as a result, was the scene of frequent skirmishes between the opposing sides. The future King Macbeth of Scotland (featured in Shakespeare's 'Scottish play') was born in the town around 1005.

By the 13th century the Norse had gone home and Dingwall was under the control of the Scottish kings. Alexander II created the town a Royal Burgh in 1226, a status confirmed by King James III towards the end of the 15th century. The original Dingwall Castle was built during the 12th century, and was at the time the largest castle in Scotland north of Stirling. During the Scottish Wars of Independence, the Castle was garrisoned by Edward I's English army but the Earl of Ross recaptured it for Robert the Bruce, fought alongside Bruce at Bannockburn in 1314 and was granted ownership of the Castle by the grateful Bruce, who was by then King Robert I of Scotland.

In 1438 Alexander, Lord of the Isles, became Earl of Ross but his son John entered into secret dealings with the English, and King James III discovered this. The King confiscated the Earldom, although the Earls of Ross were permitted to retain the Lordship of the Isles. The Castle became a royal possession but was abandoned by the Crown in 1600 and fell into ruin.

Tulloch Castle, on the northern outskirts of Dingwall, was built in the 16th century as the home of the Bain and then the Davidson families. It also gradually fell into disrepair but was restored and became a hospital for those injured during the evacuation of Dunkirk, and is today a hotel and conference centre. Stories persist of a secret tunnel, now collapsed, connecting the old Castle and Tulloch Castle.

As was the case with virtually every other part of the Highlands, the people of Dingwall and Easter Ross were badly affected by The Clearances. In 1792, starting at Strathrusdale, about six miles to the east of Dingwall, crofters across Easter Ross began to round up all the sheep in the area and started moving them, as a protest against their lands being confiscated by the new tenant sheep owners. The alarmed landlords gathered in Dingwall and wrote to the government for its assistance, admitting 'we are incapable of resistance'.

In August that year three companies of soldiers arrived in Dingwall and crushed the rebellion. That year, 1792, became known as 'Bliadhna nan Caorach', or 'The Year of the Sheep'. A similar uprising in the Dingwall area was again halted by the British State in 1854.

However, Dingwall was by now prospering economically, and its growth in trade and agriculture led in 1843 to its elevation as a 'county town'. Its new status was enhanced further in 1865 by the arrival of the railway, linking the town to the Far North Line to Wick in Caithness and to the line leading to Kyle of Lochalsh and the Western Isles. In more recent years Dingwall's economy has been boosted by the town's proximity to the nearby Invergordon aluminium smelter, closed in 1981, and the North Sea oil industry, established in the early 1970s and which continues to bring much-needed economic benefits to the Highlands.

Dingwall is also keeping pace with modern technological developments. The Dingwall Wind Co-op, launched in 2013, runs a 250KW wind turbine on the hills to the south of the town. It is the first fully co-operatively owned wind development company in Scotland.

Dingwall is an ideal centre for outdoor activities and tourism, offering in its surrounding area facilities for fishing, golf, hillwalking, watersports, cycling and birdwatching. It is also home to Ross County football club, who play at Victoria Park. The twice-annual derby League matches against Inverness Caledonian Thistle, 15 miles to the south, are known as 'El Kessocko', as many fans cross the Kessock Bridge in Inverness to and from Dingwall to attend the games.

The 'Staggies'

If you have the chance, this admittedly biased correspondent would urge you to pay a visit to the home of Ross County Football Club. Everything about County is picturesque and slightly eccentric: including a connection ('albeit a rather tenuous one', says Rab) to the world's greatest footballer.

The ground, formally named the Global Energy Stadium but known to most of the rest of us as Victoria Park, is situated just over a small hump-backed railway bridge very near the centre of town and close to the Highland Football Academy. The Club's nickname is the 'Staggies', taken from their badge, which is a Caberfeidh, or Stag's Head. This in turn was taken from the regimental badge of the Seaforth Highlanders, the regiment in which many locals fought and died during World War I. This nickname has resulted in the appearance of some very unfortunate horned 'onesies' on County's bigger away expeditions.

Few were bigger than County's expedition to Hampden to play Celtic – and defeat them 2-0 – in 2010. Still then a First Division side, County took 7,000 supporters to Glasgow to watch them beat Neil Lennon's side, and qualify for the Scottish Cup Final against Dundee United.

For that Final, there were 17,000 County fans in the national stadium. Dingwall's population is under 6,000. Unfortunately, the Staggies were gubbed 3-0 by their Premier League opponents on the day. But I can assure you that the two sets of fans joined in raucous celebration all across Glasgow for the rest of that evening. I know. I was one of them.

Ross County followed neighbours Inverness Caley Thistle into the senior set-up, and tracked them all the way up the leagues. When they were finally promoted to the top tier, they embarked on a run of 40 games undefeated before and after that promotion. But the biggest achievement of all came in March 2016, when they travelled to Hampden once again, and defeated Hibernian in an extremely nervous Scottish League Cup final. They capped a satisfying season by squeezing into the league Top Six on the last possible Saturday.

This being the Highlands, here's another footballing connection – between Dingwall and Lionel Messi's birthplace (this is the tenuous bit, Rab). Dingwall man Colin Bain Calder is buried at St Clement's graveyard in the Highland town. But he is remembered too in Rosario, Argentina, as a footballing trailblazer. Colin Calder was born in 1860, and went to Rosario City in Santa Fe Province to work for the Central Argentine Railway. He subsequently helped found Rosario Central Football Club and became its first president, in 1889. His great-great grandson still lives in Rosario.

In 1903, the club changed its name to Club Atlético Rosario Central. Barcelona's Lionel Messi, who played for local rivals Newell's Old Boys, was born in Rosario, while Mario Kempes, the man whose goals won the World Cup for Argentina in 1978, and won him the tournament's Golden Boot, played for Rosario. So far, there hasn't been a friendly... though it has been suggested.

Dingwall was for some time a major meeting point for travelling folk, though then they might have been referred to as 'gypsies', or even 'tinkers'. You will, though, have to search quite extensively to find evidence of this on official sources. But the Dingwall dialect, in which local males cheerfully describe each other as 'gadgies', still contains a lot of Romany words.

This may be why their rivals from over the Kessock Bridge used to sing 'the wheels of your house go round and round' at Ross County fans, till the humourless authorities banned as many interesting football songs as they could think of. The County fans never seemed to mind, anyway.

Finally, inside Victoria Park, the local end is not your Kop or South Bank, or anything else either militaristic or scenic. The County fans take their seats these days in what is known as the Jail End: because that end of the ground backs on to what was, until recently, the local court and remand facilities. It was to this building that Skye Bridge protesters were brought to be tried, but we'll get to that in the Kyle of Lochalsh article in this book.

Dingwall contains several fascinating places of interest for the visitor and tourist alike.

The Dingwall Heritage Trail, lasting about one and a half hours, includes the Town House with the old Tollbooth and Museum, the 500-year-old Mercat Cross, the Dingwall Canal designed by Thomas Telford and Castle Doocot (a 'folly' dating back to 1825).

There is also the Hector MacDonald Memorial, which was erected in 1907 in honour of local soldier 'Fighting Mac', whose controversial life is here examined by Iain.

Fightin' Mac

The monument to Fightin' Mac – General Sir Hector Macdonald – is one hundred feet high representation of a story of Victorian rags-to-riches-to-rags, taking in military triumphs across the world, only to end in scandal and suicide, and Elvis Presley-style sightings.

Hector Macdonald was born at Rootfield near Dingwall in 1853, the Gaelic-speaking son of a crofter, and enlisted in the Gordon Highlanders at the age of seventeen, at Fort George near Inverness.

In Afghanistan, he was offered the rare choice of a Victoria Cross or a commission in the regiment, to recognise his bravery. He chose the latter.

Then in 1885, he was part of the Nile Expedition which used small boats to get to Khartoum in Sudan, but ended in failure – arriving two days after General Charles Gordon and his garrison were killed by Islamist troops, led by the Mahdi. It was 1898's Battle of Omdurman that made Fightin' Mac a household name in this country. His men defied the Dervishes and saved Kitchener's force. Each of his men had two rounds of ammunition left when the battle ended.

In 1902, he was posted to Ceylon, now Sri Lanka. He offended the exile population by drilling the local militia – mostly the sons of British tea planters – mercilessly. He shouted at the governor to get off his parade ground and preferred to mix with the locals, rather than the Brits.

Just how much mixing he was allegedly doing emerged, with claims that he was enjoying illicit relationships with a number of Sinhalese boys. He was sent back to Blighty by the very governor he'd shouted at.

The king, on his arrival home, suggested he shoot himself....and subsequently that's just what he did, in a Paris hotel, while on his way to face a court martial.

Still, thirty thousand turned up to pay their respects at his funeral. Subsequently, a government commission reported no evidence against Sir Hector, whom they described as "so brave, so fearless, so glorious and unparalleled a hero."

It's here the frankly fanciful dragging in of Elvis Presley comes in. Just as the Pelvis has frequently been sighted in exotic places since his death, so was Fightin' Mac. He was supposedly spotted in Manchuria: at breakfast in Shanghai, and was even said to have taken the identity of a dead German general, and fought against British troops, during the First World War.

Today, there's the Dingwall monument and another at Mulbuie on the Black Isle. Robert W. Service – the creator of "The Shooting Of Dan MacGrew", among others – wrote a poem "Fighting Mac", and the doyen of fiddle players J Scott Skinner wrote a tune, "Hector the Hero".

If you stumble across a Highland celidh in your time here, there's every chance you'll hear it played.

On the first Saturday of every September the town holds the Great Feil Maree ('feil' being Gaelic for a 'fair' or 'market'), and the Feis Rois offers education and courses in traditional music, song, dance and drama. As in many Highland towns, music is an important aspect of the local culture. However, the citizenry missed out in a big way in early January 1963, as Iain explains in the poignant piece which follows.

The Fab Four

As you wander about Dingwall High Street, stop to have a look at the former tollbooth, now Dingwall Town Hall and Museum. You'll spot a small Highland Council plaque which proclaims 'The Beatles Played Here: 4th January 1963'. And so they did. To 19 people.

The trouble was that nobody had ever heard of John, Paul, George and Ringo in those days. And just up the road, at the main dance hall in the area, the Strathpeffer Pavilion, the Melotones were playing. No contest. The Melotones drew 1200, and most of those at Dingwall only went to the Town Hall because they didn't think they'd get into the 'Pav'. The Beatles, fresh from Hamburg and Liverpool, apparently didn't seem phased by the tiny attendance Still in their Hamburg uniforms – long leather jackets, drainpipe jeans and winkle picker boots – they laughed and joked between numbers with those who were there.

I know this story because there was a reunion of the audience (sadly, no Beatles came) in April 2011, and I talked to some of that audience 48 years on. Few of them were starstruck at the time, but a matter of weeks later, the Beatles released 'Please Please Me'. The rest is hysteria.

In subsequent years, I worked for one of the Wilson brothers who headed up the Melotones. I was writing a pop music column, and Willie hardly ever boasted about that January night at all. No, really...

One last curiosity: when the audience reassembled in 2011, it appeared to have grown. Two dozen turned up, claiming to have been there the first time.

I am sure that the inhabitants of Dingwall would agree that it is not the most beautiful town in the Highlands. However, the people are pleasant and friendly, and Dingwall sits in the centre of a historically important and physically imposing hinterland. It's well worth a visit.

DORES:

GAZING DOWN THE GREAT GLEN

I remember, as a teenager, pushing a clapped-out old 175cc Triumph Tigress scooter up and down the nine-mile-long hilly straight road from Dores to Inverness, and thinking that, if I ever saw Dores again, it would be far too soon.

However, the following day, with the clutch plate now fixed, I drove back to Dores, one of my favourite places in the Highlands, carried my pint of McEwans round to the open space behind the Dores Inn, stood on the old wooden steamboat pier, gazed south in the direction of Fort Augustus just over 20 miles away down Loch Ness, and thought that life doesn't get much better than this.

There was a capriciously light breeze, it was (unusually) a gloriously sunny day, and the 1,000-feet-high hills of the Great Glen swooped down to merge into the impenetrable waters of the Loch. I was so transfixed by the serenity and splendour of the scene, and by my own utter insignificance in the scheme of things, that I had to buy another pint (or maybe I had two or three more) so I could luxuriate in one of the most overwhelming and inspirational views in Scotland.

I drove my wobbly old two-wheeler back to my family home in Inverness, congratulating myself on my good fortune in living so close to such a grand wee village as Dores.

Dores (from the Gaelic 'duras', meaning 'black wood') consists of a small bunch of houses, a Parish Hall and, of course, the Dores Inn. The hamlet sits at the extreme north-eastern corner of Loch Ness, on the opposite side of the Loch to where begins the River Ness and the final stage of the Caledonian Canal, both drfting towards Inverness and the Beauly Firth.

It is bisected by what today is the B862, the Hanoverian General Wade's road to Fort Augustus, built after 1715 to keep in order the unruly, troublesome

Highland peasants. Ironically, its main use over the years was to act as a conduit for the ragged, ferocious Jacobite army who headed south in 1745 for the sole purpose of being unruly and causing as much trouble as they could.

A long, shingle beach, heading west from the village, runs along the northern shore of Loch Ness, while behind the beach lie the flat fields of Drumashie Moor. As youngsters, we used to pitch our tents just behind the beach in the summer, and make use of the facilities, notably, if possible, the Dores Inn.

Swimming in Loch Ness is out of the question, as the water is freezing. No one has yet been able to establish its exact depth, due to its overlapping rock shelves being something of an impediment to sonic measurement, but it's very deep (at least 800 feet) and therefore extremely cold. If you're sailing, try not to fall in, as you will very quickly regret it (if you can scramble out of the water in time).

If you come from Inverness, eventually and inevitably someone is going to ask: 'have you ever seen the Loch Ness Monster?' I haven't, and nor has anyone I know, but that doesn't mean it doesn't exist. I haven't seen Alpha Centauri either, but apparently that exists, so what do I know? A guy called Steve Feltham has been living since 1991 in a converted mobile library next to the Loch, and even he hasn't got any proof either way. However, some people have resorted to rather devious methods of establishing the beastie's existence.

Iain provides, in the following article, an account of one such fellow.

Frank The Fraudster

Whatever the truth about Nessie, it's transparently true that the legend of the monster, as well as the money and the publicity it promises, has attracted some truly fantastic frauds.

The most notorious was carried out by a short-tempered former soldier called Frank Searle. Wounded in Palestine, he left the Forces and became a greengrocer in London, where he read a book about Nessie, which argued that there definitely was a monster, and it was probably a plesiosaur stranded by land shifts in the prehistoric era. Not pausing to wonder how it could have survived for so long, Frank sold up and headed north. He lived in a loch-side tent and a caravan at various stages, and spent long hours looking through binoculars for proof of the monster. Then he simply started making it up.

From about 1972, he began producing photographs. They were blurred, grey and shot from a distance, but they finished up again and again in the newspapers with the usual tagline: Is This Nessie? To which the sub-editors who made up the pages would cheerfully have responded: 'No, of course it isn't: but, hey, it sells papers'.

Those who paid particular attention to Mr Searle's activities say that he took to buying postcards showing artists' impressions of dinosaurs. Hey presto, a little later another Nessie snap would appear in the popular prints.

But at the same time, real scientists were moving in to study the Loch. The American lawyer, musician, inventor and cryptozoologist Dr Robert Rines introduced sonar soundings. After a number of exhaustive sweeps of the Loch, he eventually finished up by taking underwater photos that were better, or at least more believable, than anything old Frank had managed.

Searle retaliated with ever more fantastic fakes. One even appeared to feature a UFO visiting Nessie. However, in the end, Scotland's Sunday Mail *newspaper demonstrated how Frank had made up a picture using a dinosaur from a postcard, and it was pretty much all over. A petrol bomb was flung at one of Frank's critics, though nobody was ever prosecuted.*

Searle left the Loch in the early 1980s, allegedly to go on a treasure hunting expedition. But when a film maker tried to track him down a few years later, he discovered Frank had died just a few weeks earlier in a bedsit in Fleetwood in Lancashire. Frank was a fake. But he added to the gaiety of nations, and newspapers, at least for a while.

All this Nessie business aside, and so far as one can discover, little of any historical consequence has ever occurred in Dores, which has been quite content to ignore the world over the centuries. And why not? Even today, when the area around Inverness is heaving with tourist attractions, there is little to do in Dores, apart from horse riding and hillwalking (and, of course, visiting the Dores Inn).

Industry of a sort took place in the first half of the 20th century when a large brick smokestack was erected to service a nearby tree-felling business, but its use was discontinued before 1939. It was subsequently demolished during World War II, in case a Luftwaffe bomber crew, on its way home from attempting to flatten London Docks, happened to be sightseeing in the area and thought the smokestack might have been a hitherto unknown part of Loch Ness's war effort.

In the early 20th century Mary Watts, wife of the Symbolist painter George Watts, opened an arts and crafts pottery in Dores but this was demolished in 1950 to make way for the new Parish Hall. Dores' artistic heritage was briefly reborn in the summer of 2010 when a homeless artist, known as Dr Geebers, stayed for several weeks in a tent near the Loch and created on the beach a stone sculpture of Nessie. Other local characters included 'Dave the Cave', also known as 'Dancin' with Midgies', a harmless hermit who dwelt in a nearby cave and who didn't do very much. Dores does appear to to attract harmless eccentrics.

However, the peace and tranquility which Dores had consistently maintained over the years was ear-blastingly shattered in June 2006 when the first Rockness Festival took place at Clunes Farm, just to the north of the village. Although between 1970 and 1992 Led Zeppelin lead guitarist Jimmy Page had owned Boleskine House, once home to the High Priest of the Occult Aleisteir Crowley and situated ten miles or so south of Dores, he rarely lived there, and the influence of rock music had historically been absent from the village (unless one includes my mates and I belting out Small Faces hits from our tents in the early hours).

Rockness soon changed that. During its eight years of existence (it was cancelled in 2014 and again in 2015), the music festival attracted thousands of music fans to listen to such performers as Fatboy Slim, Manic Street Preachers, Kasabian, Chemical Brothers and Mumford & Sons. In 2013, the organisers sold 30,000 tickets, but the land now seems to be reverting to its original arable state.

I now turn, with relish, to The Dores Inn. This is a cosy but fairly spacious bar and restaurant set back a bit from the road, and has always been a major attraction for both locals and tourists. I recall being served alcohol there when I was 15 years old but was refused service (by the same bar staff) the following year on the grounds that I was too young. I didn't feel it was wise to protest overmuch.

The food and beer are excellent and universally praised. Indeed, the establishment is listed in the top fifty of the *Lonely Planet* guide and is described as being one of Europe's most 'undiscovered and overlooked destinations'.

The road south from Dores to Fort Augustus, passing through such attractive villages as Inverfarigaig, Foyers and Whitebridge, mainly follows Loch Ness, with the rugged moorland and small lochans keeping you company on the eastward side. Most of the southbound traffic from Inverness makes use of the wider, straighter A82 on the Loch's western opposite side, so you almost have this road to yourself.

It's worth stopping off at Foyers, if only to have a look at the Falls of Foyers, a 140-feet waterfall plunging dramatically into a gorge leading into Loch Ness, and which is the subject of a poem by Rabbie Burns, which begins:

> 'Among the heathy hills and ragged woods
> The roaring Foyers pours his mossy floods'

It's a joyful, life-affirming litle trip, which reveals the natural, untamed landscape so typical of this part of the Central Highlands. If you didn't know that Dores was there, you might easily miss it. But you really should visit this apparently anonymous but delightful wee place.

DORNOCH:

SEA, GOLF AND MADONNA

Nestling comfortably in the fertile farming lands of the south-east corner of Sutherland, just off the main A9 and where the the Firth meets the North Sea, the small town of Dornoch is about as close as you'll get in the Northern Highlands to a conventional seaside holiday resort.

Dornoch radiates a cosy, content, almost self-satisfied air, and I don't mean this unkindly. On my (irregular) visits, it reminds me of when I used to peer into my grannie's front room when she had 'guests'. These were all 'proper' ladies, but not above a bit of gossip and, as they talked, they perched primly on their chairs, knees tightly together while brushing imaginary biscuit crumbs off their tweed skirts with rapid, fussy little sweeping movements of their hands. This, of course, is a fanciful comparison, but it captures the essentially bourgeois, rather formal feel of the place: for me, anyway.

A wide sandy beach stretches along the Moray Firth for around five miles, ambling north from Dornoch Point, nodding politely as it passes Dornoch and adopting a brisker, more spirited attitude as it nears the Loch Fleet Nature Reserve. So, with this on the town's doorstep, its relative seclusion, its unusually mild climate and its panoramic sea views, it's hardly surprising that Dornoch attracts the tourists.

The fact that this settlement of little more than 1,000 inhabitants is also home to one of the world's finest golf courses helps to boost the number of visitors. And it's a peaceful, if somewhat sleepy, place, but with an intriguing history which can be traced back at least 1,000 years to its time as a border post between the territory ruled by the Norse Earls and the lands of the emerging monarchy of Scotland.

The town's name derives from 'dorn' (Gaelic for 'fist' or 'pebble') and 'ach' ('field'). The first Earl of Sutherland built Dornoch Cathedral. The Bishop of Caithness's two predecessors had been murdered at the original cathedral further north in Halkirk, so it was clearly time to move south, away from the lands of the Sinclairs. The new Cathedral was inaugurated with a service in 1239. However, the Cathedral and many other buildings (such as the original Bishop's Palace, now the Dornoch Castle Hotel) were badly damaged by fire during a clan feud in 1570 between the Earls of Sutherland and Caithness.

In 1655 Royalists occupied the town, used the building as stables and set it alight when they retreated, leaving it without a roof and with little else. During the 1745 Jacobite Rebellion both sides in the conflict occupied Dornoch (obviously not at the same time), and the Cathedral was again used as stables. Attempts were made over the years to repair the building, but it was not until the 1830s, after the death of the First Duke, that the Countess of Sutherland undertook extensive restoration work.

In the early 20th century new stained glass windows were donated in memory of Andrew Carnegie, who was then the owner of nearby Skibo Castle. Today, it is the smallest cathedral in Scotland but nonetheless a handsome building (although being of the Protestant persuasion it's technically not a 'cathedral'). Despite its long eventful history, the Cathedral is probably best known internationally as being the venue in 2000 for pop singer Madonna's wedding.

A starstruck Iain was there to report on the high jinks.

Like A Virgin

Ah, Madonna. December 21 and 22 in the year 2000. What a truly ludicrous experience all that was.

*The pub quiz question of the hour was (and is): where did Madonna marry Guy Ritchie, who is now her last husband but one? The answer is **not** Dornoch Cathedral. The reason many people may well think that was the venue is that the Cathedral was the only place where Madonna and her (then) new man were seen in public throughout the entire three-day circus.*

Madonna's four-month-old son Rocco was, in fact, christened in the Cathedral. The northern nuptials were conducted, and possibly even consummated, in the very private confines of the Carnegie Club at the 'exclusive' Skibo Castle, where local staff have to sign a confidentiality contract if they want to work there.

As a spectacle, though, Dornoch Cathedral was where it was at. Around a thousand members of the media from all over the world congregated on the patch of grass outside the Cathedral's main doors, some of them there a couple of days before anything was due to happen. And yes, I was also there, among a forest of photographers' stepladders.

The reward for all that waiting around was a 30-second pose by mother, baby and dad on the front steps of the Cathedral. Before all that, there were hours and hours of celeb spotting, where basically most of us saw Sting, who had been heard rehearsing an aria in the Cathedral the night before, along with Mrs Sting, who is otherwise Trudi Styler; Stella McCartney, who had designed one of three different wedding dresses for the following day; Gwyneth Paltrow, an actress; and Spud. And thereby hangs a tale.

Spud, aka Calum Fraser, who lived in Grantown-on-Spey, made his name as a piper who often played nearly in tune on drink-fuelled Tartan Army escapades across Europe and beyond. When Madonna and Guy Ritchie landed in a private jet at Inverness's Dalcross Airport the day before the christening, there was Spud playing 'Like A Virgin': perhaps not the most appropriate choice.

Madonna liked it: so much so that Spud was invited to play at the Cathedral. And then he was invited to join Madge on her next inter-continental tour. But just as worldwide fame beckoned, he was dumped. Some other piper turned up to play the Scottish segment of the set, leaving Spud feeling less than chipper. Mind you, he might have been relieved to have been spared the rough side of Rab Wallace's tongue. Wallace, Head of the College of Piping, said the replacement piper was 'gallivanting around like a peat bog fairy'. His kilt was also an affront to Highland dress, he said.

Aside from Spud's undoubtedly exemplary behaviour, there was some regrettable conduct by my fellow hacks and others vaguely related to the media. There was Richard Bacon, drummed out of 'Blue Peter' for using powdery substances just a couple of years earlier, and en route to rehabilitating himself with the 'Big Breakfast' on telly. His crew were ejected from the grounds of Skibo Castle after an ill-advised attempt to infiltrate the place.

An English security guard topped that by managing to smuggle himself and a video camera into the Cathedral's organ loft. He stayed there for five days, having supplied himself with food and drink, though nobody ever explained to me how he dealt with 'comfort breaks'. I'm sort of glad about that. In any event, the gentleman, who presumably planned to sell his footage to the highest bidder, was caught by police, trying to slip out of the church after the ceremony. The local Sheriff presiding over his subsequent trial unsportingly ordered the tape to be destroyed.

The excitement, though, was considerable, unlike the non-event outside the gates of Skibo Castle the following day. The wedding took place very firmly behind the walls, as television reporters breathlessly commentated on the arrival of yet another of Skibo's black Range Rovers, mostly empty, and always bereft of star names. Brad Pitt was meanwhile supposedly spotted buying a packet of fags in Inverness, and George Clooney was said to have stayed, quietly and completely undetected, in nearby Bonar Bridge.

Inside, we learned that the groom wore a Hunting Mackintosh kilt and the bride a sash of the same tartan, while the guests were treated to a smoked salmon and haggis champagne reception followed by a ceilidh with singing, dancing and Scottish music.

I have to admit that I still suspect some of my fellow hacks of just making stuff up during the whole hysterical episode. But I have to concede I will not be casting the first stone. In my undoubtedly over-excited state, I at one point astonished BBC Scotland radio listeners by marrying Maradonna off to Guy Ritchie. The Hand of God, no doubt.

However, the locals didn't seem particularly bothered about their brief brush with superstardom. Under the heading 'Dornoch Unfazed By Madonna Hype', the *Telegraph* quoted an unimpressed resident: 'I don't know why everybody's bothering. Everybody's a singer here on a Friday night.' Well said, sir: let's get this in its proper perspective.

A less heralded event in the history of the town occurred nearly 300 years before the Madge non-fest. Iain, who is something of an expert on the subject of witches as well as on international pop stars, relates below how an extremely unsavoury and inhuman event took place in Dornoch all these years ago.

Season of the Witch

Dornoch may have several claims to fame. But one it could probably do without is its notoriety of being the last place in Britain to burn someone for being a 'witch'.

The unfortunate woman's name may (or may not) have been Janet Horne. There's a stone commemorating her death in Littletown, just south of the town's square, although the date given is 1722, when it should be 1727.

Details are sketchy but, just as the Enlightenment was driving Scotland to the forefront of European philosophy and rational thought, the old woman was being coated in tar and put to the flames, having apparently sealed her fate by stumbling over the words of the Lord's Prayer during her trial, thus proving her undoubted guilt.

Initially, her neighbours complained that the old lady, who some historians believe was suffering from senility, was guilty of devilish practices. They claimed she turned her daughter into a pony and rode her to the Devil to have her shod. Her daughter was said to have a deformity of the hands.

The sheriff depute of Sutherland, Captain David Ross, had the mother and daughter brought before him. He found them both guilty, sentencing them to be burnt at the stake the next day. The daughter seems somehow to have escaped, but her mother was stripped, marched through the town, covered in tar and finally burnt in the square. She's said to have warmed her hands at the very blaze that was about to consume her.

It's not clear if Janet Horne was her real name, as Janet (or Jenny) Horne seems to have been a generic name for witches in the north of Scotland at the time. Nine years after her death, the Witchcraft Acts were repealed. Her story was commemorated in a play called 'The Last Witch', by Rona Munro, which was performed at the Edinburgh International Festival in 2009. However, please rest at ease. These days, people in Dornoch generally don't burn anybody.

Visitors are attracted to Dornoch by the beaches, the climate and the congenial environment, but it's a reasonable assumption that a good number come here to play the Championship course at Royal Dornoch Golf Club. After St Andrews and Leith, it's the world's third-oldest golf course. Golf was first played here in 1616, according to records although the club was not formed until 1877, becoming 'Royal' in 1906. The Club is celebrating 400 years of golf in Dornoch in 2016.

It is also the world's most northerly Championship course but it has never hosted an Open Championship, partly due to the difficulties involved in fitting into such a small, hilly area vast crowds of spectators, TV crews and so on.

However, it is regarded by many professionals as one of the world's finest courses, usually ranked in the global top ten. It was designed by Old Tom Morris who won the Open four times in the 1860s, and it's a 'testing' links course (I found it absolutely terrifying) with a glorious view of the North Sea, thick rough, narrow fairways and very deep bunkers.

In the late 19th century, local boy Donald Ross was appointed head greenkeeper and professional, and he subsequently became one of the world's great golf course architects. The University of the Highlands and Islands today offers a degree in golf management, which might come in handy after (or, better still, before) playing this particularly fiendish course.

A couple of miles north of Dornoch sits the village of Embo where evidence exists of Bronze Age settlement. It's difficult today to believe that it was the site of a ferocious battle between the Norse and Scots in the 13th century, but that's what happened. Embo susequently became a small fishing port but is now another beachside resort. On 16 July 1988, Embo declared itself an independent state, in order to raise money for a community centre. They established a 'customs post' and issued their own currency, the 'cuddie', an Old Scots word for a donkey. Embo is unofficially twinned with Hawaii, although you'll struggle to find any resemblance.

The village also contains a popular holiday park: 'Granny's Heilan' Hame'. To give you a flavour of the place, here is a verse of the song from which the park's name is taken:

> 'I can still see old granny, a smile on her face
> Just as sweet as the heather dew
> When I kissed her good bye, wi' a tear in her eye
> Said, laddie, may god bless you'.

There you are. Don't you feel better already?

A short walk further up the beach brings you to the Nature Reserve on the estuary tidal basin of the River Fleet, with its sand dunes, coastal heathland and pinewoods. The mudflats are home to waders, wildfowl and seals, with oyster catchers, buzzards and ospreys wheeling about overhead, while inland you'll find pine martens, red squirrels and deer. To the south of this sea loch are the ruins of an old 13th-century keep, Skelbo Castle, long since abandoned to nature.

To reach the town from the south, cross the new A9 concrete bridge over the Firth, take a right on the A949 for half a mile, and you're there. A rail connection was opened in 1902 to the Far North Line via the Mound but it was shut in 1960. There is also a small, ex-RAF grass strip airfield south of the town, which is only suitable for small private planes, several of the passengers no doubt heading for the Skibo Castle Hotel on the other side of the A9.

Skibo Castle

The first record of Skibo Castle, located just to the west of Dornoch, is in a charter from 1211. From its early history, the Castle was a residence of the Bishops of Caithness. until 1545, when the estate was given to one John Gray in order to reinforce its alliance with a powerful family.

In 1745, Robert Gray surrendered the estate. Its ownership changed hands frequently until 1872, when it was bought by Evan Charles Sutherland-Walker, who extended the house and improved the grounds. In 1897, wealthy industrialist Andrew Carnegie took a one-year lease, with an option to buy. In 1898 he exercised that option for £85,000. However, the Castle's condition had declined so much by this time that a further £2 million was spent on improvements, including the creation of Loch Ospisdale and an 18-hole golf course.

Skibo stayed with the Carnegie family until 1982. It was later purchased by Peter de Savary and used as the foundation of a private and 'exclusive' members club: the Carnegie Club. The establishment of the Club required the restoration of the Castle, in order to recreate the luxury of an Edwardian sporting estate. De Savary sold the club in 2003 for £23million.

In 2006, a BBC Television programme featured a family who for several generations had been tenants of a farm on Skibo estate. The programme highlighted their search for a new farm following their eviction by the estate: the return of the Skibo Clearances? In 2008, Skibo became a 'members only' club (much to the relief of everyone who's not an 'exclusive' member).

And what else? As with several other small towns in the area, there is an annual Highland Gathering every August, preceded in Dornoch by the mid-July second-hand and antiquarian Book Fair and succeeded by the town's Festival Week. There are also plenty of other smaller-scale cultural events to be found here.

If your taste in holidays runs to the wild and depraved, then perhaps you should avoid Dornoch as you may find it somewhat on the tame side. But if you're up for peace, quiet, sandcastles and the bracing sea air, this is just the place for you. It really is a rather lovely wee part of the world.

DRUMNADROCHIT:
THE CASTLE AND THE MONSTER

'When sore in heart and low in pocket
Make your way to Drumnadrochit
Better door ye canna' knock at
Than the one in Drumnadrochit
Though there may be folk who mock it
No one ever asks what o'clock it
Ever is
In Drumnadrochit'

Do these stirring lines not bring a tear to your eye? Possibly composed by the world-renowned Scottish 'poet' William McGonagall, this is the opening verse in an elegaic tribute to Drumnadrochit, a village some 13 miles south of Inverness on the A82 road which follows the western shore of Loch Ness.

'Drum', as locals refer to the village, derives from the Gaelic 'Druim na Drochaid', meaning 'ridge of the bridge', the 'bridge' crossing the River Enrick which flows down through Glen Urquhart and the village to Urquhart Bay, an inlet on Loch Ness. It is overlooked by Craig Monie ('Creagh Mhonaidh'), a mountain named after a Norse prince in the 10th century who fled up Glen Urquhart to escape a battle. He was killed at Corriemony some miles up the Glen, and a stone marks his place of death.

Drumnadrochit is a tidy, pleasant little place, with its white-harled houses overlooking a village green which is turned into a riot of yellow by daffodils in the Spring. As with Fort Augustus, Drumnadrochit is on the Great Glen Way and is perfect for walking, cycling, hill climbing, dinghy sailing and fishing. Or you can jump on one of the cruise boats, such as the Inverness-based Jacobite

Cruises, which travel up and down the Loch making regular stops at places of interest during their trips. However, please do not try to break the world water speed record. This would be a mistake. Racing driver John Cobb was killed attempting just that on Loch Ness opposite Drumnadrochit in 1952.

Drum is also home to Glenurquhart Shinty Club. Similar in some respects to hockey, but infinitely more full-blooded and bellicose, shinty is a sport of Celtic antiquity and is popular in the Highlands, particularly in the west of the region. It's an exciting, if scary, game to watch but I've always been too timid to play it, leaving it to brawny crofters. Another local attraction is the Glenurquhart Highland Gathering and Games, held every August in the village.

If, after watching all this activity you feel like a rest, then try sampling some of the finest food in the area at the Loch Ness Inn (the Lewiston Arms, as was) in the heart of Drum. You could also try the Loch Ness Brewery ales, including 'lightNess', hoppyNess' or 'wilderNess'. They may even sell 'nessieNess', but I've never asked,

On the southern edge of Drum sits the hamlet of Lewiston, a planned village created in 1769 and which is close to Castle Urquhart further on down the A82. Building works in the area in early 2015 revealed fragments of skeletal human remains, a wrist guard for use with a bow and arrow and shards of pottery, all of which date back to the Early Bronze Age, nearly 4,500 years ago. Given its sheltered location and the relatively fertile land around Drumnadrochit, it is unsurprising that human habitation has long been a feature of the area.

Castle Urquhart...

The ruins of a site of more recent historical relevance stand a couple of miles south of Drum. Castle Urquhart was once a formidable defensive fortress jutting into Loch Ness, and was one of the largest mediaeval stone castles in Scotland. Due to its important strategic position guarding the main route through the Highlands, Castle Urquhart has had a turbulent history.

There was probably a Pictish fort on this site in the 6th century, and King Alexander II occupied the Castle in the 13th century. During the wars of Wallace and Bruce, the Castle was twice occupied by the English – in 1296 and 1303 – and was recaptured by the Scots in 1308. In the 1390s the MacDonalds, the Lords of the Isles, attacked the Castle, and its occupation transferred back and fore over the following 150 years, attacked again in 1545 by various West Coast clans.

The building saw its last action in 1689, when supporters of the new Protestant monarchy of William and Mary held off a siege by a larger, but less capable, Jacobite force. When the Protestant garrison left, they blew up the Castle. It then lay abandoned for almost 300 years.

A Visitor Centre opened in 2002 under the auspices of Historic Scotland, and the Castle has been refurbished. It now has its own car park, and contains a restaurant, cinema and shop selling imitation mediaeval relics. Its attractions include a recreation of a trebuchet (a siege weapon used in the days before cannon), the water gate with access to a pier and Grant Tower, the best-preserved part of the Castle. Also, you should not miss the excellent audio/visual show at the cinema: and there is much more.

Castle Urquhart is now a Scheduled Ancient Monument and, after Edinburgh and Stirling Castles, is today the third most-visited castle in Scotland. And the view from the Castle northward up Loch Ness is not to be missed.

... and The Monster

This dramatic reminder of Scotland's history, however, does not begin to explain why the village of Drumnadrochit is so crowded during the summer months.

The principal reason for the tourist coaches, the cameras and the crowds of tourists is that Urquhart Bay is regarded as the haunt of 'Nessie', the Loch Ness Monster, as its waters are probably the deepest in Loch Ness and therefore the most likely home for the supposed creature.

The existence of Nessie was first suggested in 1933 when the *Inverness Courier* printed a story of a sighting of an unusual beastie in the Loch under the headline 'Strange Spectacle on Loch Ness'. A year later a London doctor produced a photograph of a creature with an identifiable head and a long neck in the waters of Loch Ness. 'Nessie Mania' was born and continues today, even though the photo was exposed in the 1990s as almost certainly a fake.

When I was a kid, I frequently travelled up and down Loch Ness and camped on the shore, but I saw nothing unusual so I may have missed the beast. However, although there are many people who feel, as I do, that the whole thing is a harmless myth, one cannot be certain. Whether or not the animal exists is a matter of speculation, but what is beyond dispute is the welcome publicity and worldwide recognition that 'Nessie' over the years has brought to Loch Ness and the Inverness area generally.

This explains the presence in Drumnadrochit of both Nessieland, containing photos, press cuttings, audio-visual material and models of the Monster, and The Loch Ness Centre, the latter promoting itself as 'a portal to the unique phenomenon that is Loch Ness', and offering 'exhibitions about the geological formation of Loch Ness and its legendary monster'.

However, all has not been harmony between the two organisations.

Monster Wars ...

Visit Drumnadrochit, and you might think the Loch Ness Monster is either a fascinating mystery or a comparatively harmless piece of fun that has made a few local businesses a few quid.

But the truth is Nessie has caused some of the fiercest rows imaginable in this lochside village. First, there's the centres. Drive into Drum and you will come on the Official Loch Ness Exhibition, just a couple of hundred yards into the village.

Continue a couple of hundred yards further and you will find yourself at Nessieland Castle: the attraction formerly known as the Original Loch Ness Exhibition.

A row has rumbled on for many years between these tourist venues, and in 2011 it culminated in a court action. Robbie Bremner, owner of the five-star Official Exhibition, accused Donald Skinner, the boss of the Other Place, of stealing his business, and sued for over a million pounds. He alleged that Mr Skinner had defaced one of his signs, and was using similar colour schemes to the Official site, in order to pinch their visitors. There was an out-of-court-settlement, and Mr Skinner agreed to stop calling his business the Original Exhibition. He renamed it Nessieland Castle. But it would be seriously stretching a point to say that peace broke out.

In 2013, Mr Skinner put up a sign opposite his rival attraction, indicating Nessieland was 300 yards further on. Mr Bremner's team stuck one of their own signs in front of it. Mr Skinner complained. When the Bremners did nothing about it, he 'took custody' – his phrase – of their sign. He was interviewed and charged by the police with theft.

There have, over the years, been more sightings of Nessie than there has been of an end to this Monster war of words. Which one should you visit? I'm afraid you're on your own on this one. I have to live here...

A further round of 'Nessie Wars' occurred in 2013. Insults were exchanged. Businessmen stomped out of the local Chamber of Commerce. And once again the Official Loch Ness Exhibition and its neighbour, Nessieland Castle, were to the forefront.

... and more Monster Wars

George Edwards, who operates a Loch Ness cruiser out of Nessieland Castle, began the new round of hostilities when he criticised veteran Nessie researcher Adrian Shine, who's based at the Official Centre. 'Just about every time Mr Shine appears on the media', said Mr Edwards, 'he talks about a "big wave" or a "big fish"'. Mr Shine, he said, was doing a disservice to the Nessie Industry, by talking the monster down. He wrote to 70 members of the village's Chamber of Commerce suggesting that they buy Mr Shine a one-way ticket to 'wherever he came from'.

Mr Shine, who's actually been researching the monster for something like 20 years, hit back, saying his business was booming, while Mr Edwards' was failing. He also claimed that Mr Edwards actually didn't believe in the monster. Various people on either side of the argument pitched in. There were resignations from the Chamber of Commerce, and the ripples from this row continue to spread.

Such was the worldwide interest in all these shenanigans that at one point I found myself on the Loch, aboard Mr Edwards' cruise boat, recording his views for a special programme on the subject, broadcast by CBC in Canada. And on that programme, too, a row immediately took place. So, decide for yourself...

Drumnadrochit is less than half an hour's drive from Inverness, although the slow-moving caravans during the summer can make the journey feel significantly longer. The scenery around Drum is breathtaking, with the steep hills and mountains rolling down majestically to the still, deep waters of Loch Ness.

If you find yourself in Inverness, and you are sore in heart or low in pocket, you really should make your way to Drumnadrochit.

DUNVEGAN:

THE MACLEODS OF SKYE

To reach this isolated settlement of a few hundred hardy 'skeenucks' (an affectionate Highland term for inhabitants of the Isle of Skye), you'll have to drive west from Portree for just over 20 miles on the winding coastal A850, windscreen wipers at maximum speed, till you arrive at Loch Dunvegan where, at the foot of this imposing Atlantic inlet, awaits your destination.

Its Gaelic name is 'Dun Bheagain', 'dun' being Celtic for 'fort', while the 'vegan' bit has long been a subject of etymological dispute, although it does not seem to refer to dietary preferences. It may derive from the Gaelic for 'small' or 'not many', from a 10th-century Norse chieftain called 'Began', or from the Old Gaelic personal name 'Beccan'.

Whatever its origin, it is now Dunvegan and is a fairly typical, if increasingly trendy and tourist-oriented, Highland village. Dunvegan Castle is its main selling point. It's been the home of the chief of the Clan MacLeod since the 13th century, and it's regarded as the oldest residence in Scotland to have been occupied continuously by the same family.

Misty Murder

Skye is referred to in some tourist literature as 'the Misty Isle'. This, in turn, borrows from the Gaelic name 'Eilean a'Cheo' which translates as 'island of the smoke'. And if you come across the island when one of these transatlantic sea mists comes drifting in, you'll see Skye all but vanish before your eyes.

Catch it on a clear day, though, and this island is one of the most stunning assemblings of spectacular and dramatic scenery anywhere on Scotland's western seaboard. If the phrase 'God is a Sgianach' (the original Gaelic word from which my esteemed co-writer colleague derives his 'skeenucks') is not well known, it's because the natives of this 'nearly' island (there's a bridge to the mainland these days) choose not to share it with you. Then again, that's only my view, and I'm from a different island.

Dunvegan, and the land surrounding it, forms one of the most dramatic backdrops in the entire island. And it's also a place with a history, both ancient and modern. If, for example, you drive a little bit north of Dunvegan, heading towards Waternish Point, you'll come to the end of the road at Trumpan Church. There's a good walk out to the point and the lighthouse but, right here, the ruined church tells a story that looms large in the history of clan warfare.

In 1577, almost 400 members of the Macdonald clan had been massacred by the Macleods, who ruled over Skye at the time, in a cave on the nearby island of Eigg. The Macdonalds wanted payback, and at Trumpan they got it. As the local Macleods were attending the church one Sunday the following year, an army of Macdonalds from Uist landed in Ardmore Bay. They barricaded the doors of the church, then torched the building's thatch roof. Every Macleod in the church was burned alive, except for one young girl who's said to have squeezed through a narrow window and ran to raise the alarm.

The Macleods unfurled their fail-safe 'fairy flag' (see my esteemed colleague's text), gathered a force together and, in their turn, they massacred the Macdonalds, throwing their bodies in a ditch in an incident that came to be known as 'the Spoiling Of the Dyke (or ditch)'. It certainly wouldn't have been much good for drainage, you'd think.

Today, music has replaced massacres, as Dunvegan is home to the renowned Celtic fusion band Peatbog Faeries, recipients of acclaim from the folk music community worldwide. (Some other modern musicians associated with Skye include Donovan, who has a house in Portree and has named his daughter Skye, and Ian Anderson, leader of 1960s/70s band Jethro Tull, who owned the Strathaird estate to the south of the island.) Dunvegan's musical heritage is a proud one, as it was the birthplace of Donald MacCrimmon (1570-1640) who perfected the 'pibroch', and particularly the Great Highland Bagpipes, as a musical genre and who was the progenitor of the legendary piping dynasty of that name.

Dunvegan's cultural diversity is emphasised by the Giant MacAskill Museum which celebrates the life of Angus Mor Macaskill, born in Dunvegan in 1825 and dying in his adopted country of Canada in 1863. The tallest Scotsman who ever lived – seven foot nine inches tall with an 80-inch chest – 'Black Angus' could lift a full-grown horse over a four-foot-high fence with the same nonchalant ease as he could pick up a quarter-gill of whisky. Although his manner was a gentle, kindly one, he was probably not someone with whom one would wish to enter into serious disputation. He toured the circuses of North America with PT Barnum and Tom Thumb, and apparently impressed Queen Victoria (in what way, I know not).

Another local attraction is the village's Colbost Croft Museum. This is a two-roomed cottage with a couple of outhouses, and it leaves the visitor with an unvarnished impression of the miserable, peat-choked conditions in which the peasants lived in the late 17th century. The romantic mythology focuses on noble clan warriors in large castles, but poverty and destitution were for centuries endemic in the North-West Highlands and Islands.

The savage depredation of The Clearances only made matters worse for the peasants. In 1739, MacLeod of Dunvegan drove 100 of his clan onto a boat bound for Pennsylvania, although such was the public outcry in the Lowlands that the ship was stopped at an Irish port and its passengers released.

Also, in the 50 or so years leading up to the passing of the 1886 Crofters Act which guaranteed security of tenure and fair rents for the inhabitants of the Highlands, it is estimated that the MacLeods forcibly removed over 2,000 people from their lands in Skye. Sheep farming and profit obviously took precedence over 'duthchas', an almost untranslatable Gaelic word for the centuries-old mutual kinsmanship between the clan 'family' and their chief.

A couple of miles to the south of Dunvegan rears the unmistakeable shape of Healabhal Mhor, one of two flat-topped, cloud-covered mountains known as 'MacLeod's Tables', on the summits of which the MacLeod chieftains periodically gathered for celebrations at no doubt chilly and extremely wet ceilidhs. Being staunchly anti-Jacobite, they probably had a 'hoolie' (party) there to mark the Hanoverian slaughter of the Jacobites at Culloden. They certainly fought in the battle alongside the government forces under the banner of the Independent Highland Companies.

The Castle, a mile up the road from the village, was once entirely encircled by the ocean but today it stands on a rocky outcrop. The existing incarnation retains some of its 13th-century architectural inheritance, but it was built in

1840 and is a typical example of early-Victorian 'Highlandism'. The slightly unreal atmosphere of the place is emphasised by five acres of well-maintained formal gardens, more reminiscent of Surrey than of the surrounding wilderness.

The main historical attraction in the Castle is the 'Fairy Flag', a piece of cloth reputedly given to a MacLeod chief by his fairy wife and which, when unfurled, ensures victory for the clan, although it is more likely it was 'borrowed' from a Saracen during the Crusades. Visitors have included luminaries such as Walter Scott, Samuel Johnson, Flora MacDonald and our current monarch, all of whom seem to have enjoyed the Castle and its gardens.

Mountains For Sale

As noted in Rab's text, the Macleods maintain clan supremacy round these parts, and also a distinct sense of ownership and entitlement. Never was that more dramatically demonstrated than in 1997, when the 29th clan chief of the Macleods announced he was putting a mountain range up for sale.

John Macleod of Macleod was a part-time opera singer from southern climes. Indeed, he wasn't even born a Macleod. His original name was John Wolridge-Gordon, but he changed it by deed poll at the age of 16, and was subsequently recognised as the clan chief by the Lord Lyon King of Arms in 1976. His mother was the daughter of the previous chief, Dame Flora Macleod. The Eton-educated clan chief announced that Dunvegan Castle needed urgent repairs, and he was flogging off the Black Cuillins for a modest asking price of ten million quid, to pay for the tradespersons and their services. It was even reported that a wealthy American was interested. All hell broke loose.

Not only did just about every resident of Skye, and their representatives on Highland Council, and in both the Scottish and Westminster parliaments, oppose the sale. Every person who ever put climbing boot to cliff piled in against the very notion. The Cuillins are among the most popular climbing destinations in all of the West Highlands and hugely iconic landmarks to boot. And, anyway, argued islanders and climbing folk alike, the mountains didn't belong to Macleod. Ancient documents claiming to establish ownership were waved angrily about. Parliamentary motions were tabled. There was talk of sit-ins on the mountains. The Ramblers' Association threatened to invade something or other.

Three years later, the chief beat a retreat. The mountains were taken off the market.

A deal was agreed for the Scottish government, via their Highland development agency Highlands and Islands Enterprise (HIE), to take over the Castle, while the Macleod continued to reside there, and the ownership of the Cuillins would pass to the public. But even that deal didn't work out. HIE subsequently announced that the Castle would need nineteen million spent on it to refurbish it, and that price ticket was just too rich for its blood. Subsequently, a big grant application was whacked into the National Lottery, and some restoration has taken place. Nothing definitive has ever emerged as to who exactly owns the Black Cuilins.

John Macleod of Macleod died in 2007, and was succeeded by his son, Hugh Magnus Macleod. His entitlement to the chieftainship, though, continues to be disputed by an Australian, Guy Macleod, who claims descent from another Skye chief, Macleod of Talisker, and who asks, not unreasonably you might think: 'How can John have been chief of the Macleods, when he wasn't even a Macleod?' On his death, John Macleod is reported to have left an estate worth £15 million, one of the biggest legacies in Scottish legal history. And all without selling a single mountain.

Dunvegan is fortunate in the breathtaking splendour of its natural setting. If the weather is fair (don't bet on it), you can set off on some remarkably scenic and invigorating walks: from 1,000-feet-high cliffs to coral sand beaches.

There is a thriving and raucous seal colony close to the Castle; elegant and haughty peregrines, sea eagles, golden eagles and herons swoop and soar in the mist and rain; and there are even occasional boat trips to St Kilda, the forbidding, uninhabited archipelago and bird sanctuary 40 miles to the west of North Uist. The sailing trips invoke the period in the late 19th century when Dunvegan was a busy re-fuelling port for steamers heading from Oban and Glasgow to Stornoway.

'Oh, the far Cuillins...'

Should you need to know this, the highest of the Black Cuillins is Sgurr Alasdair. And the classic two-day traverse of the entire Range is said to begin at the camping ground in Glenbrittle and finish at the bar of the Sligachan Hotel in central Skye.

The Cuillins have also featured in a well-regarded Gaelic movie 'Seachd: The Inaccessible Pinnacle'; in an epic poem by the great Gaelic poet Sorley Maclean; in the execrable shortbread song 'The Road to the Isles'; in a Val McDermid murder mystery; John Buchan's 'Mr Standfast'; and even (sort of) in a Jethro Tull song. Skye band Run Rig's 'Nightfall On Marsco' may be the best of all, though.

It's well worth spending some time in one of the numerous, well-appointed B&Bs and hotels, but it's not the sort of area in which one would expect to find an award-winning, Michelin-starred restaurant.

However, The Three Chimneys, across the Loch in Colbost, is just that, having opened in 1984 and it has won more than 30 major awards for the quality of its food. Frank Bruni, the influential New York restaurant critic, named it in 2004 as one of his top five restaurants worldwide.

Waternish Point

If walking's your thing, you can head out to Waternish Point, though it's a sometimes boggy route that passes the remains of a couple of Iron Age brochs (defensive forts), one of them still containing a short covered walkway. At the end of this walk, which is likely to take you several hours, you'll come on the lighthouse at Waternish Point which, like many Highland light towers, is not only automatic, but also solar-powered. And yet it still works at night. Ah, the wonders of science.

The other wonder at Waternish Point is, simply, the view. If this part of the island isn't living up to its nicknames, you can see all the way down the coast here, and out to the Outer Hebrides. Minke whales gambol in the manner of a frisky double-decker bus in the waters in between. Skye can be stunning.

So Dunvegan is certainly an intriguing place, as you might expect. But watch out in August. This is Skye and therefore an ideal breeding ground for midgies. You don't want to make their acquaintance. You will regret it.

FORT AUGUSTUS:
THE ABBEY VILLAGE

As an energetic, enthusiastic teenager in the 1960s I once foolishly signed up for a sponsored 34-mile charity walk, which involved setting off at midnight from the centre of Inverness and walking the length of Loch Ness along its western shore.

As I neared the conclusion of this heroic walk some 12 hours later, I felt like a character in one of the old Greek philosopher Zeno's paradoxes: the closer I approached journey's end, the further away it seemed. When I finally arrived I have rarely been quite so exhausted nor have I felt so relieved to lie down. However, despite my labours, I harbour no ill will whatsoever towards my ultimate destination: the welcoming and attractive village of Fort Augustus.

There are two roads leading from Inverness to Fort Augustus: the western, more popular one and the eastern one, which Iain here describes.

The Other Loch Road

As outlined here by Rab, the village of Fort Augustus is a placid and pleasant place, especially the centre of the settlement around the old bridge, which manages to include a big petrol station and a sprawling car park, and still somehow look attractive. But one of its hidden treasures is the way to get there... at least from Inverness.

The B852 will carry you on a twisting, undulating route from the Great Satan at the mouth of the Caley Canal, taking in many passing places – be aware, we are not talking Route 66 here – through some of the most iconic of Highland landscapes. I'd go as far as to say it's one of my favourite Highland driving routes, though by no means the quickest, unless you're stuck behind a convoy of caravans, mobile homes and trucks on the opposite bank at the height of the summer. My advice in these circumstances: go east, young man (or woman, indeed).

What you get on the east bank of Loch Ness is the Highlands In Miniature. Here is my route plan. Head out towards Dores on the lochside. This road will take you through avenues of trees, past a primary school apparently situated in the middle of nowhere, and then to Dores. Here you can choose to go on towards Foyers and other lochside settlements. I would advise taking a left (this is not a political statement), and heading up into the hills above Loch Ness.

As you climb through the trees again, look out for oncoming traffic, because the road layout is a little eccentric and you need to know where your next passing place is. You will be rewarded at the top of the hill by a panoramic look out over the Loch, but be careful where you park. Among the places over on your left (though just out of sight) is Loch Duntelchaig, from which Inverness still gets a lot of its water supply.

On the onward route, there's an RSPB reserve on your left at Loch Ruthven. It is peaceful and, on a good day, beautiful. Surrounded by sedge and birch wood, its major attraction for those of a twitching propensity is the rare Slavonian grebe, which, says the society, 'looks its best (in early spring) in gorgeous red and golden plumage, the jewel of the Highland Lochs'. The RSPB also reckons you can see ospreys, diving birds and toads. Some eating the others, no doubt. And in the winter, flocking tits in the wood. Really. It's also important to note there are hides here, but no toilets.

As you rove on southwards, you drive through moor and hill and viewpoint, past blue lochs and everything you've ever imagined about the Highlands. You might even feel the need to take some pictures. In among this scenic delight, you'll come to Loch Tarff, which is a very bonny stretch of water, described on one website I've seen recently, as having a beach just big enough for a rug, and a small car parking area. And, enthuses the writer, you can swim out to the little islands offshore. I have to admit this is on a blog site dedicated to outdoor swimming, but if that's your thing...

Along the way, you'll pass through stretched-out settlements alongside the road, like Errogie and Ardachy and Whitebridge, which is pretty much a hotel and some Shetland ponies in a field (at least the last time I was there). Just off the road, it is reputed, there are places like Knockcarrach, Moor of Knockchoilum and Bunkegivie. I have no idea if these places exist, but their names are magnificence enough.

Take this road. You won't regret it.

With a permanent population of only around 400, but a magnet for 300,000 visitors per annum, Fort Augustus is clearly a popular tourist venue. It sits at the foot of Loch Ness, roughly halfway along the Great Glen ('An Gleann Mor' in Gaelic), the geological fault line which divides the Highlands and Lowlands of Scotland, and where the River Oich accompanies the Caledonian Canal in the direction of Loch Ness. The Canal was built by Thomas Telford and completed in 1822 at a cost of twice its original budget. It connects Fort William at its southern end, via Lochs Lochy, Oich and Ness, with the Highland Capital of Inverness and the Moray Firth to its north.

The Canal is an engineering triumph, raising boats up 60 feet through eight locks, known as 'Neptune's Staircase', from Loch Linnhe at the southern end. At Fort Augustus, five locks lower boats over 40 feet from the Canal, bringing them down to the level of Loch Ness, the last nine miles being a flat run from the northern end of Loch Ness, via another few locks in Inverness, to the Beauly Firth and the North Sea. The Canal was partially funded by the British government in order to move warships quickly from coast to coast to counter potential threats of invasion by the French.

It is now a Scheduled Ancient Monument. You can also visit the Caledonian Canal Visitor Centre in Fort Augustus if you happen to be a canal obsessive (these people do exist). Cruise boats operate up and down Loch Ness, including Jacobite Cruises, an enterprise created by my late father in the early 1970s. The trip down the Loch is a humbling but also an uplifting experience as you drift past some of the world's most arresting and majestic scenery.

Until the early 18th century Fort Augustus was known as Kiliwhimin, which derives either from St Cummein, the Abbot of Iona who built a church here in the 7th century, or from the 13th-century Ku Chuimein, an abbot of the then all-powerful Comyn (later Cumming) clan. The Comyn's influence declined after Robert the Bruce murdered the chief, 'Red' John Comyn, at a church in Dumfries, and Bruce had to go into hiding in caves and look at spiders.

After the 1715 Jacobite Rebellion, Hanoverian engineer General Wade built a fort here, and it was named after the Duke of Cumberland, William Augustus, who terminated the 1745 Jacobite uprising in April 1746 at Culloden, his massacre of injured Jacobites and innocent civilians earning him the soubriquet of 'Butcher' Cumberland. Wade had wished, understandably if a touch hubristically, to call the fort and settlement Wadesbridge, but his fellow Redcoats vetoed this plan in favour of Cumberland.

In May 1746, after Culloden, Cumberland moved to Fort Augustus. He then unleashed another reign of terror on the surrounding areas, killing and plundering irrespective of whether the inhabitants had or had not supported the Jacobites. He brought his booty back to Fort Augustus and turned his temporary headquarters briefly into Scotland's largest cattle mart, in one year putting up 20,000 cattle for sale.

In 1867 the fort was sold to the Lovat family, the Frasers, who nine years later passed on the fort and land to the Benedictine Order of monks. By 1880 the Benedictines ('the black monks') had built Fort Augustus Abbey and an upper-class public school, marking the restoration of monasticism to Scotland. It was an imposing if somewhat incongruous building, given its setting in the shadow of the rugged Monadhliath Mountains, Gaelic for 'Grey Mountains'.

The Abbey closed in 1993, due to educational enrolment problems (and a good thing too, as there are far too many public schools in Scotland). The building then briefly became the largest private exhibition centre in Scotland, but was sold five years later and has now been converted into private apartments. In 2013 a group of former pupils made allegations of serious sexual and physical abuse by some of the monks. The Church apologised but investigations continue into this murky episode.

Fort Augustus was connected by rail from 1903 to Spean Bridge, linking the village with Fort William and the south, but the line was closed in 1933. The village sits on the winding A82, which follows the Glen on its western side: a busy road in summer, but a frustratingly tedious trek if you're stuck behind an obdurate caravan or one of the many slow-moving tourist coaches, both of which routinely ignore the pull-in passing places.

The wide, salmon-rich River Oich runs through Fort Augustus, and is traversed by Old Oich Bridge, a B listed, 19th-century wooden structure, now closed to traffic. There is an established six-mile walk along the river. The village is also on the Great Glen Way, opened in 2002, and used by cyclists and walkers on its 73-mile meander from Fort William to Inverness.

The Great Glen Way is Scotland's fourth Long Distance Walking Route. It is normally walked or cycled from the south-west to the north-east, following the prevailing wind and with the sun (yes, 'the sun') behind the walker. A typical walk takes five to six days and you can cycle it in around three days. After Fort Augustus, the Way veers up into the forest above Loch Ness.

Dam All To See Here

The other considerable landmark on the Other Road is Glendoe, situated just above Fort Augustus. This is the mother and father of recent Highland Hydro developments. Owned by SSE, the idea of Glendoe was to bore a hole through a mountain to drop the water from one dammed Highland loch to a pumping station much lower down, on the banks of Loch Ness, producing enough electricity to supply a large city like Glasgow with around five per cent of its annual needs.

The head drop at Glendoe (excuse the tekky speak: it basically means how far the water has to run downhill from the reservoir to the turbine station) is the highest in the UK, at 600 metres. The tunnels to bring the water downhill were drilled out by a giant boring machine, which was named by local school children, in one of these faintly embarrassing PR exercises, Eliza Jane. The 200-metre-long machine took two years to bore its way through the hills.

Watching the thing break through rock at the end of the main tunnel's excavation was definitely dramatic, and somehow reminded me of the science fiction movie 'Dune'. Which you probably haven't seen. Now it's done, most of this is all but invisible from the road.

The point about all this Highland hyperbole is that this was one of the largest of Scotland's civil engineering projects, and was officially opened by the Queen in 2009. I was there, but She didn't speak to me.

I did, though, get to interview the boss of SSE for breakfast radio live in the grounds of a Fort Augustus hotel. He seemed to think it would last forever. Weeks later, it closed. Rock falls within the tunnel meant the whole scheme had to shut down for major repairs and safety checks. It took three years to bring it back online. SSE sued the German company who built the tunnel for thirty million quid. Which tends to put your quarterly electricity bill into context.

As one might expect, Fort Augustus is not short of hotels, B&Bs and self-catering apartments: perfect for a quick stagger back from the 'ceilidhs' which occur every summer, or from the local golf course which is supposedly the most challenging nine-holer in Scotland. And there are plenty of friendly bars and decent restaurants in the village and surrounding area. It all sounds pretty idyllic and, as the village is relatively sheltered, the weather is mild by Highland standards.

Also, if you're concerned about midgies, a quick glance at the website midgieforecast.co.uk gives you regular updates on their presence in Fort Augustus (or anywhere else, for that matter), on a scale of 1 to 5. A score of 1 indicates their relative absence, but 5 will probably lead to the breakdown of your marriage, such is the mayhem these wee beasties can cause. You'll be relieved to know that Fort Augustus is normally 1. I'm not sure if this site isn't a joke, but it seems serious enough. You can even download an iPhone app from the site, which should help break the ice at your dinner party.

If your vacation tastes tend towards all-night, ecstasy-fuelled, Ibiza-style raves, then you can forget this wee place. But if you're more inclined to peace, quiet, gazing at the Loch or tramping the shinin' heather, then you could do a lot worse than Fort Augustus, splendid place that it is.

GAIRLOCH:
JEWEL OF THE WEST COAST

Without wishing to sound like an over-enthusiastic spokesperson for the local tourist board, I have to say that the small town of Gairloch is located in what is the most peaceful and visitor-friendly landscapes in the Western Highlands of Scotland.

Sitting on the shore of Loch Gairloch ('the short loch') in Wester Ross, the town faces the northern tip of Skye and is surrounded by imposing mountains, secluded lochs and sandy beaches. The area has a permanent population of around 1,000, and is an irresistible destination for visitors and tourists, attracted by its scenery, wildlife, fishing and weather. It's on the North Atlantic Drift and enjoys a warm microclimate, with a higher than average annual rainfall,which ensures a rich and diverse variety of plants, animals and sea life.

Redpoint Ramble

Speaking as a Highlander, Gairloch is one of these places that seems a long way away if you're sitting somewhere like Inverness, but always turns out to be worth the trip.

You head first for Ullapool on the A835 then, having passed through the village of Garve, with its large hotel that seems to be repainted regularly (a singer-songwriter friend of mine wrote a song in praise of Garve, but then had to keep changing the words, as the hotel kept changing hues), turn leftwards for Achnasheen on the A832.

This road takes you past a couple of viewpoints looking across the mountains to the rapidly approaching West Coast, before you swing left by Kinlochewe, and head on past the beautiful Loch Maree, possibly pausing at the Victoria Falls (yes, really), which are perhaps not as spectacular as their African namesake. However, situated within Slattadale Forest, they are impressive enough in their own wee way.

Quite often, I get this far – and just a little bit further – and then I don't go to Gairloch at all, or at least not till a lot later. Just as you think you're nearly there, you'll come across an old hump-backed bridge on a road off to the left, signposted for places like Badachro and Redpoint. Take it.

Down the B8056 (these numbers are getting larger and longer and possibly denote a certain lowering of expectations of the route), you're heading into another of the Highlands' better-kept secrets. Down this road, there are countless boat anchorages and, tied up to them are loads of craft of all persuasions: dinghies, creel fishing boats, yachts and, occasionally, full-on gin palaces. This is to be seen at fullest effect from the agreeable frontage of the Badachro Inn, where locals and yachties foregather, drink, chat and occasionally understand one another, while gazing out at a bay littered with boats. And the food's good.

Carry on down the road, by way of hamlets with natty names like Opinan, South Erradale and Port Henderson, and you come eventually to Redpoint. This is one of my favourite beaches in a place that has lots of them. The name comes from the coppery colour of the sand on the beach, above which stands yet another spectacular viewpoint with a cairn to keep you properly aligned as you look west into the heart of the Isle of Skye.

There are parking places at Redpoint, and from your car you can choose to take a short path on the right to a relatively enclosed beach, backed by towering sand dunes. Larks go bananas as you pass across the grassland on the way to the beach in summer, while sheep munch at you in a mildly interested kind of way. There is also another bigger, lower beach with an offshore tidal island, though that requires a longer walk through farmland. If you have dogs, keep them on a lead and make sure you close the gate. Spend a sunny day at Redpoint. Then drop in for a drink at the Badachro Inn on your way back. Life will rarely seem so fine.

Another attraction of Redpoint is that while it is at the end of the road, it lies at the start of a track which runs for seven miles south-east along or above the shore to Lower Diabaig. This is a lovely walk, but you need to bear in mind when starting it that when you get to Lower Diabaig, you will be seven miles away from your car, and the shortest road distance between them, via Kinlochewe and Loch Maree, is 45 miles.

En route, you pass the remains of an old fishing station, overlooking the beach on the south side of the promontory of Red Point. Five miles from Redpoint you pass one of the Scottish Youth Hostels Association's more remote hostels at Craig.

The Iron Age fort ('An Dun') on the headland close to the town's golf club indicates the town's prehistoric origins. The Vikings used the Loch as a safe haven (the small island of Thorndale was named after Norse god Thor) until Norwegian rule ended after the Battle of Largs in 1263, when King Alexander III sent them homewards to think again.

The MacLeod and MacKenzie clans then vied for control of the area, until King James IV in 1494 granted the land to the MacKenzies and the King commissioned Hector MacKenzie, the first Chief, to destroy the MacLeods 'by fire and sword'. This draconian policy, however, obviously did not work, as there remain plenty of MacLeods around Gairloch. However, the MacKenzie family still today oversees the estate from Flowerdale House, just inland from the town.

Since they became owners over 500 years ago, the MacKenzies of Gairloch have been generally respected for their loyalty and commitment to their tenants. Unusually, they refused to evict any tenants during The Clearances, although the estate was then running at a loss. Indeed, a number of Highlanders who had been 'removed' from nearby estates settled in the Gairloch area and were accepted by their new landlords. It is difficult to think of another estate of a similar size in the Highlands which, given the land-grabbing greed of the time, adopted a similar humanitarian policy to its tenants.

The MacKenzies also decided to take no part in the 1745 Jacobite Rebellion, which proved a wise decision. In the years following the '45, thousands of Highlanders enlisted in the British Army, first for the American Revolutionary War and then for the war against Napoleon. The recruitment in the Highlands was on such a scale that in 1799 virtually all the menfolk from Gairloch were fighting for the British Army against the French.

Today, the predominantly white buildings of Gairloch straggle along the shoreline of the Loch, and the town consists of three main interconnected hamlets: Charleston, Achtercairn and Strath. To the south, Charleston contains the sombre brownstone Free Church ('Wee Free') on the hill. Also in this part of town is the harbour, which busies itself with creel shellfish and small-scale trawling,

Heading north, the lovingly maintained Heritage Museum at Auchtercairn contains, among its many other local documents and artefacts, the first Pictish stone, dating from between 500-700 AD, to have been found on the West Coast mainland. The commercial centre of Strath at the north end offers the usual collection of village shops as well as a fine view of Longa Island in the

Loch. The beach is safe and clean, although from time to time the Loch is plagued by swarms of jellyfish, so keep your eyes peeled for these irritating midgies of the ocean.

From Strath it's a fairly steep ascent to Poolewe, an attractive little village, on Loch Ewe, but the short journey is an essential one if only to visit Inverewe Garden. Created from a barren, rocky outcrop by Osgood MacKenzie in 1862, this 52-acre site is now maintained by the National Trust and is one of Scotland's most beautiful gardens, containing over 2,500 exotic plants and flowers and, when introduced, included such rarities as Himalayan blue poppies and Chinese rhododendrons.

The Stone Thief

If you do make Gairloch eventually, then I entirely support my colleague's enthusiasm for the place.

I'd recommend unreservedly one of the best book shops on the west coast of Scotland, at the Mountain Coffee Company and Bookshop, where there's a certain air of old hippy combined with mountain folk, that comes together to squeeze out good coffee, great cakes and a wide and esoteric range of stuff to read.

Among the locals – she came from Firemore, a crofting community north of Gairloch, created when crofters were cleared to the coast from the inland glens – is the woman who stole the Stone of Destiny. Kay Matheson ended her fairly eventful life as a resident of a local old folks' home in 2013. She was 84.

Back in 1950, the 22-year old domestic science teacher was recruited by a fellow nationalist 25-yearold Ian Hamilton, along with two others, to steal the Stone of Scone – on which Scottish kings had been crowned – from Westminster Abbey, where it had lain since being looted from the monastery at Scone in Perthshire by Edward I of England in 1296. British monarchs were crowned on it, emphasising their overlordship of Scotland.

Just after four o'clock on Christmas morning, the Scottish raiders broke into the abbey, leaving Kay – who had the flu – sitting lookout in a car. They somehow prised the 152 kilogramme block of red sandstone free. A policeman came to investigate at one point, but Kay and Hamilton threw themselves into an enthusiastic clinch, not only distracting the bobby from the fact that they were where they shouldn't be, but also from the scraping noise from the abbey, as their two co-conspirators dragged the stone across the floor of the abbey.

In the end they succeeded in liberating the stone – in two pieces – and some months later it turned up, draped in a saltire, at Arbroath Abbey. All four were eventually detained, but none were ever charged. While Ian Hamilton became a Queen's Council (QC) and fully formed eccentric later in life, Kay Matheson was an itinerant teacher of Gaelic and lifelong SNP supporter. In fact, she stood for the party against Charles Kennedy for her home constituency in 1983.

In 1996, the then secretary of state for Scotland Michael Forsyth decided to repatriate the stone to Scotland. Kay Matheson was the only one of the four conspirators who watched the stone arrive at Edinburgh Castle in the company of Prince Andrew.

' It was all worth it', she said.

During World War II Loch Ewe, a sheltered deepwater sea loch, was used as one of the main assembly points for the Arctic Convoys which made the perilous supply run to Murmansk and Archangel, with the U-Boats lying in wait. It is estimated that around 3,000 men lost their lives attempting what Winston Churchill described as 'the worst journey in the world'. A memorial stands at Cove commemorating these men, and there are continuing plans to establish a permanent museum to the Convoys at Aultbea on the eastern side of the Loch.

On the peninsula, which separates Lochs Gairloch and Ewe, sits the coastal village of Melvaig, and at its northern tip stands a lighthouse named Rua Reidh ('the point of flat rocks'), some 12 miles north of Gairloch, which was designed by David Stevenson, cousin of Robert Louis Stevenson.

On the opposite promontory to the east of Loch Ewe is Greenstone Point, haunt of a legendary 'water-kelpie', which apparently lived in Loch na Beiste (named after the creature) and which was described as resembling 'a good-sized boat with the keel turned up' according to a 19th-century account. So watch yourself up there, as you don't want to tangle with kelpies. A 'kelpie', incidentally, is a water demon in the shape of a horse, and the name comes from the Gaelic 'cailpeach'. meaning 'colt'. But offering it sugar lumps won't improve your survival chances.

The Ghosts of Gairloch

If you're of an energetic disposition, then I would suggest you take to the hills behind Gairloch's scenic Old Inn. There you will find as spooky a spot as I've been to. 'The Fairy Lochs' is not the sort of name you would expect for a living graveyard. Named after a nearby hill, getting to the series of small lochans above the village is a sometimes strenuous climb, but you won't forget how it ends.

High above Gairloch lie the wrecked pieces of a US Liberator aircraft. As you approach the first of the Fairy Lochs, a beautiful spot in its own right, your eyes will take some time to adjust. But yes, that really is a bit of an aero engine on a partly-submerged island in the middle of the loch.

And, yes, over there, that's burnt and broken pieces of aluminium and the ghosts of scorch marks in the heather. And here, against a cliff, wreckage – including a broken propeller – gathered up to make a shrine in the actual spot where, in 1945 after the war in Europe was over, 15 American servicemen died when their plane got lost in fog and crashed.

The Liberator had flown the men out from Prestwick Airport headed for the States and should not have been anywhere near the crash site. But they somehow flew into the peak of a mountain called Slioch near Loch Maree, then smashed into the hills above Gairloch, as the crew tried to crash-land.

Today, the memorial cairn urges people not to take souvenirs. It lists the dead and says: 'this site is their last resting place. Please treat with respect and take only memories'. The memories of the Fairy Lochs will stay with you.

The waters of The Minch, home to shoals of small fish of all shapes and sizes, also attract dolphins, porpoises and even sharks and whales, with regular boat trips from the harbour offering whale-watching expeditions.

Moving inland from Gairloch, there are in the immediate area 23 peaks of 2,000 feet or more and at least 30 fairly large freshwater lochs, the most spectacular yet tranquil being Loch Maree, surrounded by birch and pine forests.

The Loch is almost at sea level so it was probably once an ocean inlet. The song 'Loch Maree Islands' has been recorded by Calum Kennedy, Andy Stewart and a host of other kilted chanteurs.

The Gairloch Bard

Gairloch is the final resting place of the renowned Gaelic bard Uilleam Ros or William Ross (1762–1791), known as 'the Gairloch bard'. Ross was born in Broadford on Skye and travelled extensively throughout the Western Isles, becoming known for his knowledge of different varieties of Gaelic. He composed several famous romantic poems attempting to win the affection of Marion Ross of Stornoway, who apparently never responded to his attentions. Perhaps the most famous of these poems is 'Feasgar Luain'. Ross settled in the Gairloch area, became a schoolmaster, and died at the age of 28 in Badachro. It is believed that he died of a broken heart.

In this area there is also ample scope, depending on your fitness level, for walking the rocky paths and peat bogs, exploring Flowerdale and Shieldaig forests, hill and mountain climbing, trout fishing and pony trekking, while south of Gairloch in the direction of Kinlochewe is the Beinn Eighe Nature Reserve, the mountain of Beinn Eighe being Gaelic for 'file mountain' due to its distinctive shape. Closer to Loch Torridon to the west of the Reserve is Beinn Alligin ('jewelled mountain'), the most westerly of the Torridon mountain chain which contains some of the oldest rocks in the world.

Gairloch is theoretically accessible from Inverness by train, with the nearest station being at Achnasheen ('the field of storms'), although it's an energetic 30-mile stroll along the length of Loch Maree from the station to Gairloch. It's probably easier to get hold of a car and take the A832 at Garve, which will lead you to the village.

Finally, I agree most heartily with the following observations of my co-author Iain, a 'coast-wester' born and bred:

See Gairloch and you've seen the Highlands. Well, it's obviously not as simple as that, but there is more than an element of truth in it. Because Gairloch can offer a little of everything that visitors come to the Highlands to see. A typically strung-out Highland village linked historically to the sea; a superb and complex coastline that is both rocky and sandy by turn; islands; lochs; and views that include some of the best mountains anywhere.

There is so much to see in the Highlands and Islands, but you really should **not** miss Gairloch.

GOLSPIE:
'THE MANNIE' OF DUNROBIN

*"Neath the shadow of Ben Bhraggie
And Golspie's lordly stane'*

Although Daniel Defoe said it first, Benjamin Franklin is normally credited as the source of the observation that nothing in life is certain, except death and taxes.

However, had either of these admirable gentlemen travelled through East Sutherland, they could have added a third item to their brief list of existential inevitabilities (at least in a local sense), ie being unable to escape viewing the statue of the First Duke of Sutherland.

Dominating the landscape for miles around from the summit of Ben Bhraggie (rarely has a name sounded more appropriate), this 100-feet-tall memorial to hubris is impossible to miss. The Duke, who ordered the statue to be erected, was responsible for the imiserisation of at least 15,000 of his tenants, and who lived in what was, at 1.5 million acres, the largest private estate in Europe, his headquarters being the massive folly of Dunrobin Castle. He even coerced his tenants into paying for the statue's construction.

It was finished in 1834, the year after his death, as a 'tribute' from 'a mourning and grateful tenantry' to 'a judicious, kind and liberal landlord': the words carved on the foot of this excrescence, which is known throughout the area as 'the Mannie'.

There are a few misguided souls who argue that the Duke and Duchess truly believed these sentiments, and felt that they were saving the local peasantry from a life of cruel hardship. However, the truth is that the Duke was a rapacious aristocrat who cared not in the slightest for his tenants, who kicked them off their lands to make way for profitable sheep farming, and who was responsible for the very worst excesses of The Clearances.

Blow the Mannie Down

There are antidotes to the enormous egotism of Dunrobin Castle, Golspie's fine monument to cruelty and self-delusion. They are found in various places across the dead acres devastated by the Sutherland family. There's Helmsdale and Badbea, to which we'll return. And especially there's that statue – 'The Mannie' – on Ben Bhraggie.

Quite recently, there were plans to have 'the Mannie' down. Many of these were minted by SNP characters, though support came from many other parts of the political spectrum. In 1995, a planning application was even lodged with Highland Council, by Badenoch councillor Sandy Lindsay, to destroy the statue. He wanted to replace it with a Celtic cross and panels describing what happened during the Sutherland Clearances. But in the end that never happened.

Emotions still run high about 'the Mannie'. I remember a perfectly serious conversation with an otherwise rational acquaintance about how the statue was hollow and would therefore be very easy to dynamite. That never happened either: but hey, my legal advisers are still at hand.

Following the Sandy Lindsay controversy, graffiti was daubed on the statue, and in May 2010 the word 'monster' was sprayed across it in green paint. The following year, two sandstone blocks were removed from the plinth in an attempt to topple it. During the 2014 Independence Referendum campaign, it was draped in a giant saltire.

As recently as 2015, an internet petition was launched by a Lewis man, calling once again for 'the Mannie' to be taken down. It was, he suggested, akin to having a statue of Adolf Hitler in Jerusalem, and was a carbuncle on the face of the Scottish Highlands.

A Golspie man started a counter-petition to keep the Duke in place, arguing that it encouraged a discussion of 'a horrific period in Scottish history', as if there might still be two sides to the debate. But I have had a discussion with a resident of the village, whose not untypical view was that it provided a very good navigation guide for those at sea, 'and anyway we quite like it'.

But then it was the good folk of Sutherland, the inhabitants of Golspie foremost among them, who were persuaded to stump up for the thing in the first place. So be careful who you talk to in Golspie.

Golspie has the sad misfortune to sit right underneath 'the Mannie'. The Gaelic name is 'Goillspidh', but the original name derives from the Old Norse for 'gully village' or 'Kol's settlement'. It's a small coastal town, situated roughly halfway between Dornoch and Brora. It's a pleasant, friendly place, inhabited over the centuries by the usual mix of Pict, Gaels and Norse settlers who relied on the fishing trade for their livelihood. The town expanded in the 19th century to make room for the people evicted during The Clearances, with today's population hovering around 1,700 inhabitants.

The arrival of the Far North Line in 1868 brought with it visitors and tourists, attracted by the peace and quiet, the scenery, the pretty little harbour and the large sandy beach. Golspie has several other items of interest, notably the the 17th-century St Andrew's Church, the popular Golspie Inn on the main A9 heading north from the town, and the Big Burn, here described by Iain.

The Big Burn

One of the hidden delights of Golspie is the Big Burn bridge walk. It takes a little finding but, as you go up the road out of the village, heading for Dunrobin Castle, you'll see a stonemason's establishment that makes gravestones, and other similar deathly delights, off on your left, just after the Ben Bhraggie Hotel. Drive in down a signposted track and you'll find a small but perfectly serviceable car park. Don't finish up in the stonemason's. They'll think you want a gravestone.

Set off through the trees alongside the burn, and you'll see the former sawmill off to your right across the river. Ahead you'll find a towering railway arch, and you'll cross a little hump-backed crossing. Two more footbridges follow, taking you to one side of the burn, then the other. And so it continues, with rock walls towering over you, all the way to the waterfalls. In all, you have to cross the burn five times, and if you keep going straight ahead you come out on a wooden walkway to discover the hidden falls just round the corner, almost where you least expect them.

It's a remarkable all-but-secret walk (don't tell anyone) and very easy. You can make it more strenuous by retracing your journey to a set of steps heading off to the left (if you're heading for the falls: right if you're coming back), which will take you back above the cascade.

The Walk Highlands website advises then: 'Turn right at a junction and then right again a short distance further on. Ignore a path descending back into the gorge and continue ahead to pass alongside a car park. This provides an alternative start point for the walk; continue on the path directly ahead. Eventually a cross-roads of paths is reached just short of an attractive millpond. The routes ahead and to the left make a recommended loop around the millpond, an ideal spot for a picnic.'

And that's it. The Bridges of Sutherland County. Without Clint Eastwood. But still a great wee walk for all ages.

The town's golf course cannot make up its mind whether it's a links or a parkland course, but is nonetheless something of a challenge. I once played it with a friend, who had last picked up a golf club before Jack Nicklaus's voice had broken, but he had once played off a more than respectable five handicap. After his first drive had sailed into the whins, I immediately doubled the size of the bet on my victory. That was a mistake, as he hammered me: once a class golfer, always a class golfer.

Three miles to the south of Golspie is the national nature reserve of Loch Fleet, home to such wildlife as terns, wading birds and seals, while one mile to the north is the Ruritanian immensity of Dunrobin Castle, seat of the Dukes of Sutherland. Further along the road to Brora, on the seaward side of the A9, is Carn Liath (or Strathsteven) Broch, the well-preserved remains of an Iron Age stone tower built around 2,000 years ago.

Trawlin'

Golspie's long, long Main street may seem featureless if you're driving swiftly through it. But actually there are a whole succession of interesting places along the main drag. Few of them match up to The Trawler. This is arguably one of Scotland's best fish and chip establishments, aka Top Chippy.

First opened in 1964, it has gone unobserved, until recently, by those strange people who confer titles on the unlikeliest places,. But in 2015, it was finally noticed nationally, with a nomination for the regional round of the National Fish and Chips Awards. As their own website proclaims: 'even to reach this stage in the competition, our food was prepared and cooked to the highest standards and judged by industry experts, rating us on food quality and customer service'.

And they insist they'll keep on coming back till they win it. They cook scampi and scallops from the West Coast, as well as their own smoked salmon and fish cakes, not to mention vegetarian options, meat from the local butcher, and there are outdoor tables when the weather's decent. Try it out before it gets famous.

Charming place though Golspie most certainly is, there is little doubt that the area's main attraction is Dunrobin Castle. I remember once, after I had driven through Sutherland and observed the ruins of several old cottages and the relative desolation of much of the area, sitting in the formal gardens of this temple to the vanity of overweening pride, and wondering how any human being could live with the guilt of owning this massive mansion while surrounded by wretched poverty.

The sheer scale of Dunrobin is breathtaking. Well, one could reply, so was Glasgow's Hampden Park, also built close to some of Britain's poorest areas. However, Hampden was designed to accommodate 135,000 people, many of whom came from these poverty-stricken areas, while Dunrobin was home to one family who luxuriated in wealth and privilege while they sacrificed the local peasantry, for whose security and well-being they were to a great degree responsible, at the altar of profit. However, to be charitable (if one must) times move on, and that was then.

So what is Dunrobin like today? It's difficult to improve on Queen Victoria's description of the building as a 'mixture of old Scotch Castle and French chateau'. To reach the place, one must turn right off the A9 shortly after Golspie and drive through a long straight tunnel of trees to the north face of the Castle, which is, in fact, the rear of the building. The main entrance is a five-storey tower facing the North Sea and a huge planned garden.

Tours are available round the rooms, as are displays of falconry in the gardens, but you should not miss the museum, which was originally a summerhouse. As well as numerous animals' heads, shot while on safari (you can close your eyes, if you are of a sensitive disposition) and African relics, there is a superb collection of Pictish symbol stones and cross-slabs (stone grave covers) bearing designs carved over 1,500 years ago. There is also historical information on the area's geology and its coal and gold mining. It's all fascinating stuff.

The Castle's history is a typically complex Scottish tale of dynastic intermarriage, feuding, intrigue and various nefarious deeds, and is far too detailed to describe here. Suffice to say that King Malcolm I gave it to the Duffus family in 1210, and over the years it has been home mainly to the Earls of Sutherland who expanded and added sections as the centuries passed by. Most of today's building was restored in the 1840s by Sir Charles Barry, with the result that in 1851 it was three times bigger than it had been six years previously.

In the early 20th century, Sir Robert Lorimer made further refurbishments and restorations. During World Wars I and II Dunrobin was an auxiliary naval hospital, and for a few years in the 1960s it was a private boarding school. It is now again a stately private home, and by some distance the largest such residence in Scotland.

Aside from Dunrobin, the Golspie area, both coastal and inland, is ideal for all sorts of outdoor activities, as you can imagine. But be careful. 'The Mannie' is watching you, and there is no escape from his pitiless gaze.

HELMSDALE:
GOLD AND THE CLEARANCES

My mother was born and brought up in Caithness, so my brother, sister and I would pile into my father's car about four or five times a year and head north from Inverness to visit the farm and her family.

This was back in the late 1950s and early 1960s, long before the construction of the Kessock Bridge and the later bridges over the Cromarty and Dornoch Firths, so it was a long, winding journey via Dingwall, the Struie and Bonar Bridge.

I became very familiar with Helmsdale, around 30 miles south of our ultimate destination of Lybster. The Ord, the border post on the A9 to the county of Caithness, was just a few miles past Helmsdale, so I knew then that we were not far from the farm.

Helmsdale, with a current population of around 600, is an unassuming little fishing port on the North Sea coast of Sutherland and was, in the 19th century, frequently visited by some of Europe's largest herring fleets. Its name derives from the Norse 'Hjalmundal' ('Dale of the Helmet') which, in Old Scots, became 'Helmsdal'. In Gaelic it is known as 'Bun Ilidh', meaning 'foot of the river'.

In the 1st century AD the Roman senator and historian Tacitus (who must have been informed of this second-hand as he never ventured this far north) described the region as being populated by 'tall, red-headed men'. St Ninian apparently preached here in 390, and the Vikings, those rapacious Norse pirates, arrived and established a settlement in the 9th century. Even back in those days, it was a fishing port, and a prosperous one.

In the 1490s the Earl of Sutherland built a castle on the promontory where the River Helmsdale meets the sea. It was in this castle in 1567 where one Isabelle Sinclair poisoned the 11th Earl and his wife the Countess of Sutherland in an attempt to gain the Earldom for her son. Unfortunately for her, she also accidentally poisoned her son and she was condemned to death, cheating the hangman by committing suicide. This story is said to have inspired Shakespeare to write 'Hamlet'.

Helmsdale was laid out in its present form in 1814 mainly to rehouse the communities evicted from their homes in the nearby 'straths' (Gaelic for 'large river valleys') during The Clearances. The remains of the castle were demolished in the 1970s to make way for a new A9 road bridge, although Thomas Telford's bridge, completed in 1811, still spans the river in the village.

In 1869 the Helmsdale area temporarily became the Yukon of the Highlands, as gold nuggets were discovered in the adjacent Strath of Kildonan and an estimated 600 prospectors made their way to Helmsdale. They even built a settlement, Baille an Or, with its own 'saloon' but, despite the excitement generated and the *Inverness Courier* sending a 'special correspondent', the amount of gold found was too small to justify the expenditure and the 'gold rush' slowly petered out. However, enthusiasts still today pan for gold in Kildonan, swimming through the shallow waters in their wet suits.

Herr Goldenballs

'Baile an Or', the name given to the shanty town that grew up around the Kildonan Burn, translates from the Gaelic as 'town of gold'. And certainly there was, and still is, gold in them there hills and water.

I've been taken on a gold-panning exhibition in the Burn myself, though my yield was fairly pitiful. But enough gold was allegedly recovered from the Burn in the months leading up to the London Olympics to make at least one gold medal. One hopes Chris Hoy got it. A few years before that, a lovestruck young man from south of the border also managed to swill enough grains of gold out of the Burn to make engagement rings for himself and his beloved.

Until recently, you could try it yourself by hiring gold-panning equipment for a fiver a day from the Strath Ullie crafts shop, which doubled as the local tourist office. However, that shop closed in 2015, and it's not clear whether anybody will now hire you the pan and other accessories. But while it's unlikely you'll make your fortune today swilling the waters of the Kildonan Burn, the old-timers reckoned they knew how to make a buck on the back of the gold rush: none more so than a mysterious German called John Peter Dunker, aka Peter Kagenbusch, who turned up in Helmsdale in 1880 and claimed he could melt mountains to make gold.

He claimed to have invented a new process, whereby he could extract the motherlode of the gold which had appeared in the rivers from the rocks themselves. To that end, he carried large loads of boulders down the strath to a house with a furnace that he'd rented in the village, causing great excitement in the area. According to the local harbour master the rock was 'pulverised and put into conical crucibles, which are then put into a furnace and by some chemical process the gold falls down in a molten state into the short conical apex at the bottom of the crucible, and retains that shape after cooling'. He claimed to have seen a piece of gold shaped like that.

The Duke of Sutherland wanted nothing to do with Dunker, but agreed to let him take three hundred pounds out of the area around the Kildonan Burn and the neighbouring Suisgill Burn. He built two more smelters and claimed to have recovered silver as well as gold. The Duke's factor was sceptical : 'I expect he will be off some time one morning without saying goodbye to his friends at Helmsdale'.

In the end, he was off, though not before trying to send rail trucks full of rocks to one of his former hunting grounds in Leeds, then promising to transport more boulders to Glasgow, where he claimed to be trading as The Precious Metal Smelting Company and to have bought a large smelting establishment, costing over a thousand pounds (big money back then). But Mr Dunker never reappeared in Helmsdale and nor did his money. Fool's gold, you might think.

Despite the gold fever, fishing remained Helmsdale's main livelihood. The Helmsdale Ice House, a Scheduled Ancient Monument, has been preserved close to the war memorial at the mouth of the river as a tribute to those halcyon fishing days. This stonewalled structure, with a roof of soil and turf, was filled with local or Norwegian-imported ice in order to keep the fish, particularly salmon, refrigerated.

However, Helmsdale is probably best remembered or, rather, is most notorious, for being the Highland area most savagely affected by The Clearances. The Countess of Sutherland's husband, the Earl of Stafford who became the First Duke of Sutherland, 'removed' between 6,000 and 10,000 tenants from the massive estate between 1807 and 1821, with the Strath of Kildonan cleared of its inhabitants, mainly the Gunn clan, between 1813 and 1819.

The Earl's agent, the Lowlander Patrick Sellar, encountered some minor resistance from the crofters in the Strath and retaliated by destroying and burning down houses, killing many people and rendering the remainder destitute. He was tried for this vicious revenge attack but a a hand-picked jury found him not guilty of murder.

Also, from 1810 to 1825 hundreds of people from the local straths endured forced 'emigration' to Canada and New Zealand. The Emigrants Statue, on the south side of the river, commemorates these people and others like them. The inscription includes the words 'their voices will echo through the empty straths and glens of their homelands'.

The Other Statue

The ten-foot tall Clearances statue in Helmsdale was built at the mouth of the Strath of Kildonan as a direct riposte to the aforementioned 'Mannie' on the top of Ben Bhraggie above Golspie. After the attempt to obtain planning permission to remove the Duke failed, fund-raising attempts began to erect a rival construction. And finally in 2007, the then-First Minister of Scotland, Alec Salmond, unveiled 'Exiles', a creation by Gerald Laing, a Black Isle-based sculptor who had mixed with Andy Warhol and his crew back in the 1960s, and one of whose other works adorns the entrance to the English national rugby stadium at Twickenham. 'Exiles' shows a crofter looking westward to a new life, his wife gazing back to the strath they had been cleared from, and a young child, representing the future.

In the audience for that unveiling was a Canadian millionaire Dennis Macleod. It's appropriate that Macleod not only paid for the statue, but also made his fortune from gold mining across the water. Not only that, his family came from the Strath of Kildonan, emptied by the Sutherland family and their factors. There's another 'Exiles'. An identical statue has been installed on the banks of the Red River in the modern city of Winnipeg, where many of the Sutherland exiles settled after being cleared from their homelands.

Five miles north of Helmsdale, near Ousdale, are the stone remains of a former village known as Badbea, perched on the edge of the bleak, precipitous cliffs of Berriedale. During The Clearances, and beginning in 1793, it was inhabited by families kicked out of their homes in the local fertile straths of Longwell, Ousdale and Berriedale to make way for profitable sheep farming. The women had to learn weaving and spinning in their tiny crofts, while the menfolk worked as fishermen, occupations for which they were entirely unsuited.

Their children and livestock often had to be tethered by ropes to boulders or wooden posts so that they would not be blown off the cliff edge by the strong winds whipping off the North Sea. The hamlet was finally abandoned in 1911, and a monument was erected on the site as a permanent reminder of the ravages and cruelty of Badbea.

Badbea Folk

The plaque at Badbea was erected in 1912 by David M Sutherland of Wairrappa and Wellington in New Zealand, commemorating his father Alexander, born in Badbea in 1806 before leaving for the Southern hemisphere in 1839. Also commemorated are George Gunn and his wife and their eleven children. Imagine how much rope you'd need to keep all of those youngsters safe.

Most dramatic of all though, perhaps, is the plaque to John Sutherland, known as 'John Badbea', 'loved for his Christian character and the charm of his personality, and gifts as one of "the Men"', according to the panel. Though he was born at Ousdale he lived most of his life at Badbea before his death in 1884.

As almost an afterthought, this panel also commemorates John's brother Donald. He died at the Battle of Waterloo. The last tenant, it's recorded, was John Gunn, who left in 1911. Go and visit Badbea. You will marvel how people ever managed to cling to these cliffs.

This whole disgraceful episode in Scottish history was hastened to its conclusion in 1886 with the passing of the Crofters Act, a process aided by a Helmsdale man, John Fraser and others from the village. Fraser was a leading light in the land reform movement, which helped create the formation of the Highland Land League. A monument to Fraser stands in Gartymore at the south of Helmsdale. One can learn more about The Clearances in the area, and a good deal of other fascinating information about the village, by visiting the not-for-profit Timespan Heritage Museum on Dunrobin Street, which runs alongside the river.

In the Helmsdale area, as one can imagine, there is an abundance of wildlife and nature trails, while a stroll around the busy harbour, with its fishing vessels, lifeboat and pleasure craft, is a rewarding way of passing one's time. There are welcoming bars and restaurants in the village, including La Mirage, a cafe which is painted pink and which contains memorabilia of the romantic 'novelist' Barbara Cartland, who was a friend of the owner and a frequent visitor to Helmsdale.

Four miles to the south of the village you will discover a stone, erected by the Duke of Portland in 1924, which marks the last wolf killed in Sutherland, the species' eradication having occurred around 1700. Also, if you happen to be in the village on the third Saturday in August, it would be impossible, and deeply irresponsible of you, to miss the world-renowned Highland Games, featuring the Scottish Hill Race and the stirring Pipers' March through the village.

Helmsdale today is such an attractive and friendly place that it is easy to forget the callous and inhuman reasons for its speedy growth in the 19th century.

INVERNESS:
CAPITAL OF THE HIGHLANDS

In common with most people about to set off on a tour of the Highlands, it's a pretty safe bet that you'll be passing through, and quite possibly staying in, Inverness. You can't really avoid it.

Dalcross, a few miles to the east of the city, is today a busy, modern airport, serving flights from the major UK and several European cities; the main road from the south, the A9, which only a few years ago passed through the city centre, now bypasses the city but is easily accessed; the railways from the south and the east terminate here, with two smaller lines leaving for the Far North and Kyle on the West coast; and there is no shortage of affordable B&Bs and hotels.

Inverness also has the good fortune to be surrounded by some spectacular scenery. To the north the elegant, imposing Kessock Bridge soars over the Beauly Firth towards the dark hills of the Black Isle and the mountains beyond; the view south from the Castle Hill affords a panoramic view of the magnificent Great Glen; while all around sit the glens, forests, hills and moorlands of the Central Highlands.

The River Ness bisects Inverness, winding and widening its passage as it travels from the northern end of Loch Ness through the city to its destination in the Beauly Firth. There are several unusual and intriguing areas within the city, although many of the recent buildings are architecturally uninspiring, and some parts of the town, notably the area around Bridge Street and the Eastgate Shopping Centre, generate an aesthetically dissonant contrast with Inverness's largely Victorian town centre.

I was born and brought up here in the 1960s, when it was a market town containing around 30,000 inhabitants and a place where nothing very much happened, at least in my opinion. In the early 1970s I headed southward to Edinburgh then to London, where I have lived for the last 40 years or so. But every time I return for a visit I am taken aback at the changes which have occurred in my hometown.

Today, the small town which I left all those years ago is one of the fastest-growing cities in Europe, is home to almost one-third of the population of the Highland Region, and is regularly voted one of the top ten cities in which to live in the UK. The growth of Inverness in recent years has indeed been dramatic, a development linked in no small way to the economic benefits of the North Sea oil boom. Although the centre of the city remains, with some glaring exceptions, the same place it was when I lived there, culturally the city has developed remarkably.

A River Runs Through It

Despite my colleague's ambivalence about the town of his birth – and most of us suffer from that – I have to admit that, as an incomer, I've slowly developed a deep affection for the place, though I never quite forget that this is the place the Gaels used to call 'the English Town', and they didn't mean it as a compliment.

It is indeed a fantastic jumping-off point for the rest of the Highlands and Islands, and that remains one of its greatest attractions, alongside its plentiful accommodation for visitors, which ranges from self-catering flats to pretty upscale hotels.

However, let me lead you to one or two of Inverness's lesser-known gems. Come down with me to the River Ness, often fast flowing and still a magnet for summer sun worshippers, though flood defence work has made the banks a little less accessible in the centre of the city.

Out in the river, upstream from the New Bridge are the Ness Islands, which lie opposite the Bught municipal pitches, just a step or two away from the centre. They were accessible only by boat till 1828, and the original bridges were swept away in a flood 21 years later. Two suspension bridges replaced them. The islands are a little oasis of trees and sunlight. Dog walkers come here, but there's still wildlife to be seen, from ducks to otters, and even occasional seals can be spotted, hunting out in the river. Salmon fishers in voluminous waterproofs stand motionless in water up to their thighs.

Just along from the Islands there's Whin Park, which features all sorts of play facilities for children, a miniature railway you can hitch a ride on and a chance to take a row boat out on an artificial waterway.

Opposite the Bught entrance to the islands, there's also a new crazy golf course (which opened at Easter 2016). And not far from the Islands' entrance on the other bank, Bellfield Park offers tennis courts, a putting course and another kids' play park. They'll also hire you bikes.

Another surprisingly peaceful part of Inverness's city centre is to be found at the bottom end of Church Street. There's very little through traffic here, and two of its finest features are neighbouring church buildings, now doing very different jobs.

The Gaelic Church was built here in 1649, and eventually became Greyfriars Free Church. Today, much of the building is a rambling and picturesque second-hand bookshop, which stocks everything from page-turning thrillers to precious prints. With its glass-fronted book cases and general air of quiet contemplation, you could easily imagine yourself in an establishment from an earlier century.

Right next door, there's a church that is still doing more or less what it was built to do. The Old High Church was Inverness's original Parish Church, dedicated to St Mary. Built on a hillock called St Michael's Mount, a church has stood here since at least the 12th century. The base of the bell tower is reckoned to date from the 15th century, while the top half was built probably in the 17th . The present building was probably completed around 1770. But the holes in the graveyard wall can be dated very precisely. They are bullet holes. The guns that fired them belonged to red-coated Hanoverian soldiers who shot Jacobite prisoners in the graveyard after the battle of Culloden in 1746.

Just up the street, there's Abertarff House. Built in 1593, this is the earliest surviving house in Inverness. Look out for the crow-stepped gables – known as 'corbie steps'. Look out also for the Dunbar Centre, which is now a drop-in centre for senior citizens (like your two authors), but in past times was a school and a hospital, notably when cholera came to Inverness in 1849.

And if all that sightseeing is too much for you, head a little further up Church Street, and you'll find one of Inverness's finest music venues in the award winning 'Hootananny's', where you'll get Highland-style and more traditional music in the downstairs bar, and more rock-influenced events on the first floor. They also do that Highland staple, Thai food, and have won prizes for their beer.

Recently, there's been a controversy in the bar, though, based on sexual harassment. The male bar staff used to wear the kilt. But they stopped doing so, because too many of their female customers decided to establish for themselves what a real

Highlander wore under the kilt. The indignant owner described it as 'sheer sexism'. But if that's a disappointment, I can share with you the secret of what's worn under the kilt. Absolutely nothing. It's all in good working order. Don't say I'm not good to you.

Inverness's geographical location has been the dominant factor over the centuries in determining the town's establishment, growth and economic status. It is located at the northern end of the magnificent Great Glen, which is generally regarded as the cultural boundary between the Highlands and Lowlands of Scotland (although, in its geological definition, the Highland Boundary Fault runs from Helensburgh to Stonehaven, south of Aberdeen).

Inverness is where the River Ness joins the Beauly Firth, which in turn is a wide estuary of the North Sea, with its abundant fishing harvest and its easy access to trading opportunities with mainland Northern European ports, particularly in the Low Countries and the Baltic.

Inverness is also a relatively secluded spot (though sometimes it may not feel that way) and is sheltered by some of Britain's most imposing mountains. Its immediate hinterland possesses a rich fertile soil, ideal for livestock and arable farming, and its surrounding forests, grasslands and moors contain a wide variety of trees, birds and wildlife. The city's natural advantages are considerable.

The area that is now called Inverness (from the Gaelic 'Inbhir Nis': 'mouth of the river Ness') was first inhabited in the early 4th millennium BC, but historical records begin during the Pictish age, which lasted from approximately the 4th to 11th centuries AD.

The Picts were a mysterious people and they left no written accounts of themselves, but they seem to have been a well-administered military aristocracy who controlled most of Scotland and whose chief recreations were hunting, sailing and warfare. They were also highly skilled artists and craftsmen, as revealed by their legacy, found across the region, of ornate jewellery and intricately carved stone statues.

In the 6th century AD, the Pictish King Brude ruled the land of Moray, which then stretched from the Hebrides to the Moray Firth, from his castle, built on the ruins of a 4th-century BC vitrified fort on Craig Phadraig ('Patrick's rock'), one mile to the west of what is now Inverness. He was visited by St Columba who, by most accounts, converted Brude to Christianity. Under Brude's protection, farms spread down the Craig's hillsides and extended as far as the River Ness, which was then the second-fastest flowing river in what is now Britain and which was, as it is today, rich in salmon and other fish. This is where 'Inverness' was first established.

During the early Middle Ages a small settlement gradually developed on the east bank of the Ness. The river acted as an effective barrier against the occasionally aggressive clans to the west, and to the north of the settlement a harbour opened, to trade in furs, timber, salmon and herring. Shipbuilding also began to assume economic importance, as oak from the upper reaches of the Ness and fir from the adjacent River Beauly were floated down to what is now the town's Merkinch, meaning 'a flat island' and which was then a shipbuilding centre. Indeed, the flagship for the Venetian navy was built here in the 12th century, and by then the town was already establishing a reputation for its industrious and skilled workforce, including tanners, weavers, butchers, shoemakers and, of course, shipwrights.

The Picts gradually vanished from history, their extinction perhaps hastened by encroachments from other tribes and peoples or through intermarriage with the Gaels who, by the 12th century, controlled most of the Highlands.

Norse invaders began to arrive in the north of Scotland in the 9th century but their influence was minimal in Inverness, which was beginning to fall under the jurisdiction of the emerging Scots Lowland monarchy and to move away from the dominance of the Gaelic clans. These new Scots kings saw Inverness as their main base in the Highlands, they built a royal castle (the first of many) in the town, and King David I granted Inverness a Royal Charter.

By the 13th century the town was organised around four main streets (High Street, Bridge Street, Castle Street and Church Street) and the first bridge had been built across the River Ness. Craftsmen and traders from the Lowlands, England and Europe visited the town (a sizeable Flemish community already lived here), trade was brisk, and the various peoples and cultures intermingled with apparent ease.

Although by the 16th century the majority of the population was still Gaelic-speaking workers and peasants, there were also a number of wealthy merchants and businessmen who used Old Scots or English as their preferred languages.

Inverness was beginning to develop in a different direction to its Highland neighbours, most of whom remained attached to the pre-feudal Gaelic ways of clan life.

There were repeated incursions on the town by Western clans, notably those controlled by the MacDonalds, the Lords of the Isles. Parts of Inverness were often damaged by these attacks, but the invaders were usually repulsed. Situated at the confluence of several trading and travelling routes, and sitting between the lands of the warring clans, Inverness was frequently besieged and harassed by its neighbours.

As an example, in 1562 the Earl of Huntly captured the town and denied Mary Queen of Scots entrance to the castle, but she soon obtained her revenge (by hanging him). The house on Bridge Street in which Mary lived during her siege of the castle was the oldest dwelling in Inverness until, in an act of wanton civic vandalism, it was demolished in the 1960s to make way for a concrete office block.

The architectural atrocities carried out in the Bridge Street area in the name of 'modernity', including the ridiculous Victorian Castle erected in 1836 on the neighbouring hill during the romantic heyday of 'Highlandism', remain an unsightly scar on the centre of Inverness.

In the 1650s Oliver Cromwell's army occupied the town and built near the harbour a large pentagonal Citadel, capable of holding 1,000 men. After the Restoration, the building was demolished and the stones were used to build a bridge over the river. All that remains of the Citadel today is a clock tower, although its provenance has recently been the subject of dispute. There have been several main bridges over the years. The latest one (universally referred to as 'the new bridge') was erected in 1961 and replaced the fondly remembered Suspension Bridge which was built in 1855.

After the 1715 Rebellion, the Hanoverian General Wade took over responsibility for the Castle, but it was burnt to the ground by the retreating Jacobites in 1746 before they were massacred at the Battle of Culloden, four miles to the south of the town. Many Invernessians, whether or not they were supporters of the Jacobites, were savagely treated by the Duke of Cumberland's men in the aftermath of the Battle, and the town became an English garrison.

After the departure of the English army, and aside from the usual internecine clan feuds and squabbles, life in Inverness quietened down (relatively), and it became a solidly bourgeois Highland town, but one with a distinct working-class population.

Its dialect tended (and still today tends) towards a combination of the softly lilting Gaelic tongue, the influence of its English army occupiers, the arrival of English-language schoolbooks and the influx of people coming from England and Europe to settle here. The difference between the Invernessian accent and that of the settlements to the east and the west of the town is marked, and Invernessians are today reputed to speak the clearest, dialect-free English in Britain and far beyond.

Inverness, however, has always been a working town with its own phrases, words and patois, which are often incomprehensible to visitors. So, although the town prides itself on the enunciation and clarity of its spoken language, many of its inhabitants still communicate with each other in a tongue which is unique to the area.

What's 'In' A Name?

Inverness has gone by many names, and many nicknames, down the years. Inbhir-nis ('mouth of the River Ness') is the most commonly accepted Gaelic name, and an exact and fairly boring translation of the English, albeit it may have initially been the other way round. But in English, there's a variety of fairly odd nicknames. The best known of all must surely be the Sneck, Snecky or even Inver-snecky. Why, you may ask.

Well, opinions vary, but probably the most widely accepted is that an extremely 'shinin' heather' music hall singer called Harry Gordon, who was a major star in the first half of the 20th century, had a signature song 'The Laird of Inversnecky', which he trotted out on every occasion. Gordon was actually from the north-east, and for many years Aberdeen has boasted an establishment called the Inversnecky Café down on the city beach. But it's thought the name was transferred to Inverness, simply because of its similar sound.

In 2014, a nationwide survey concluded that the Sneck was the happiest place in Scotland – though it must be said it was conducted for a property company who may have had houses to sell here – and another survey came to the same conclusion in 2015. One newspaper dubbed the place 'Happytown', but I suspect that label won't stick.

For a long number of years, many Gaelic speakers dubbed the place 'the English Town', not necessarily because it was full of Sassenachs, but because the inhabitants conducted much of their business in that foreign language, even when the lingo of the hearth might still be Gaelic.

It's probably from this period that the shibboleth about Inverness natives speaking the best English in the country emerged. At the start of the 18th century, the town was said to be almost entirely Gaelic-speaking. By the end of that century, the town was said to be bilingual, and early in the 19th century, one observer said that in Inverness both languages were spoken with 'utmost purity'.

In recent years, the city fathers, mothers and other marketing types have concocted a slogan emphasising the 'In' in Inverness, if you see what I mean. Thus 'dineINverness', 'stayINverness', 'relaxINverness' etc. It's frankly INtolerable, but I suppose it's a variation on the name theme.

Then there's Polish. Poland's Consul General in the Highlands estimates that at least 5,000 Poles have come to the city seeking work. The brilliant and late lamented 'Inversnecky' website actually published a Polish phrase guide, arguing that: 'spoken by an estimated 98.4% of Church Street Co-op customers, Polish is now more widely spoken in the ~~town~~ city than English and Gaelic combined, and a grasp of at least the basic phrases of the language is essential to surviving life in the Highland Capital'. This is not true, but quite funny. And the Polish for the town/city is, it seems, Invrnesz.

As to the purity of Inverness English, well, you may be less than convinced if you come across this fairly popular doggerel:

1) *Whilst walkeen down the street today in sanny Invarness*
   I stambled on a baker's shop whose menu dudh ampress.
   I wandered in and ordered, then the weetrass said to me:
   Theres yer bahered scones, jawm donahts an yer cap o tea
2) *Now had I crossed the ruhver and gone to the West End Chapper*
   I could have bought a can uv Coke and a fine block pooodeen sapper.
   That is, of course, if I could stond the teedyass strang of text:
   'Ya waneen sol and vanagar? Enyheen else? Two eighy, NEXT!
3) *A wandered over by the Haugh down to the Bellfield Pork.*
   Where local tennas players proctas strokes from dawn til dork.

These days, their treenurs cost the earth, the soles have rabber sackers.
In my day lads wore plamsoles, and the girls punk frully knuckers
4) *So there you go, my tale of woe, it really is a putty.*
That we should change what was the town into a flameen sutty.
We should dispel that age-old rumour, source of endless anguish
When people say we are 'Best speakers of the Unglash longwudge'

So, there you have it. Just one other name that will beguile you. The broadcaster and journalist Tom Morton used to transmit a nightly programme from BBC Scotland's Broadcasting House in Inverness, where he laboured to create an alternative universe based around the city. And his name for Inverness? Well, given the proximity of marine marvels in the Beauly Firth, it was: Dolphinsludge. Can't say fairer than that.

Inverness is the administrative centre of the Highlands, and home to both the Highland Council and Highlands and Islands Enterprise (HIE), the successor to the Highlands and Islands Development Board. Its economy has long depended on fishing, agriculture, trade, light industry and tourism, assisted by Loch Ness, nine miles to the south and which is supposedly the domain of 'Nessie', the Loch Ness Monster, 'discovered' in the 1930s.

The arrival of hydroelectric power, and then the oil, stimulated an economic awakening in Inverness and the wider area. Inverness, like many of the towns along the Moray Firth, has prospered economically and has attracted thousands of new residents to take advantage of the booming economy as well as to enjoy the glorious scenery.

Do I Know You?

There have been many famous folk with connections to Inverness, though you want to be careful about accusing some of them of being Invernessians. The city's Raigmore Hospital was, and is, the Highlands' main medical facility, and many people from other places away from Inverness were born there, but didn't actually live here.

Among those are Lord Derry Irvine (of Lairg), who as Tony Blair's Lord Chancellor, spent a huge amount of your money (£650,000) on doing up his official residence. Contractors had to sign the Official Secrets Act to avoid news of the extraordinarily expensive wallpaper – £59,000 a roll – leaking out.

It did anyway, and he made a bad situation worse by defending his extravagance in front of a parliamentary committee, which was televised, dismissing the row as 'a remarkable storm in a teacup'. Alistair Campbell intervened and Lord Irvine was gagged.

Subsequently, he was sacked, and didn't even succeed in getting the job of Ambassador to Australia. Among the other stories that emerged was the one about the barrister's relationship with his senior clerk, who effectively doubled up as his butler and was seen, on one occasion, allegedly rushing to polish his boss's boots. Other famous folk from the Sneck – sort of – was another Labour figure. Yvette Cooper, born in Inverness, is famous because she was Works and Pensions Secretary in a Labour government. She also married Ed Balls. She was one of the unsuccessful candidates when Jeremy Corbyn won the leadership of the Labour Party.

Other more genuine names are Mary Macpherson, who lived in the town and is famous in Gaelic culture as 'Great Mary of the Songs'. Karen Gillan, a flame hairead actress, played Amy Pond in 'Doctor Who' and still regularly visits her home town.

And back in the 1970s, the award-winning author Ali Smith, who was born and brought up in the Dalneigh area, worked briefly as a receptionist at BBC Highland. She went on to be nominated three times, at the time of writing, for the Mann Booker Prize and to win a whole series of other awards. Back in those brief BBC days, she once lent me a Bill Withers album, which I have never given back. Sorry, Ali.

Inverness today possesses much in the way of outdoor activities, sporting events, historic sites, visitor facilities, entertainment, bars, restaurants, the widely acclaimed Eden Court Theatre, music and arts venues (including hosting rock and folk music festivals only a few miles from the town centre), major shopping outlets and a great deal more. Visitor accommodation, from grand stately homes and tower houses to hotels and bed and breakfast houses, is also plentiful.

All this information can be found in a variety of outlets, in particular the *Inverness Courier*, a local twice-weekly institution of a newspaper, which celebrates in 2017 the bicentennial year of its foundation. You may also care to consider reading my book *Snow on the Ben: A guide to the real Inverness and the Highlands*, which gives information on the town, its history and, as I mention above, its often unique local words and phrases.

Much of what constituted the 'real' Inverness (as I recall it from my youth) has disappeared in recent years, destroyed by diggers, bulldozers and town planners. In its place has arisen, in some areas, a somewhat ersatz version of the old place: an idealised version of what existed beforehand. Much of the town in which I grew up has now fallen victim to 'progress'.

The Victorian-influenced 'land o' the shinin' heather', 'Bonnie Prince Charlie' romantic stories and tales which you will have encountered are vigorously promoted in the city. However, although a good deal of this history is based on fact, much of it is invented mythology. And why not? These idealised visions and narratives of the Highlands are good for business, and we all need to survive. And generally they do no harm and often offer solace and entertainment, so long as you don't believe most of them. What we need is some futile scepticism, to paraphrase 'Monty Python'.

It's certainly true that the Inverness area and the Highlands are, in many places, wild, remote and ruggedly beautiful. However, it's also true that the variety of economic life and culture in this region is multi-faceted, unusual, intriguing and much more than a local Gaelic dreamscape. From forestry to fishing and from oil exploration to distilleries, the Inverness area and the Highlands is a fascinating and diverse region for visitors to explore.

KYLE OF LOCHALSH:
OVER THE BRIDGE TO SKYE

'When the sun has gone down on the dark western island
And the work is all done for a while
We'll gather together, whatever the weather
And we'll drive to the dancing in Kyle'

'The dark western island' to which this verse of a traditional song refers is the Isle of Skye: land of mists and mellow midgies. 'Kyle' is Kyle of Lochalsh, a settlement perched on the mainland shore less than half a mile from Skye across the waters of Loch Alsh.

The lyrics to 'The Dancing in Kyle', a grand song of which the above are the opening few lines, conjures up an image of carefree young cheuchters gliding around the village hall to the rousing accompaniment of a Hielan' dance band: a splendid and much deserved end to a day's hard toil.

Hard toil is no stranger to Western Highlanders. For over 500 years ferry boats transported cattle, people and cars from Kyle to the village of Kyleakin, on the east coast of Skye. In 1995 the ferry boat service was withdrawn and replaced by a toll bridge, under the first-ever Private Finance Initiative scheme. It was built and owned by a private company and was the only bridge in the area which drivers had to pay for the privilege of crossing. It was also believed to be the most expensive toll bridge in Europe.

Understandably, there was an outcry about this structure, with many considering it inappropriate, extravagant and worse. However, it must be said that the bridge eliminated the interminable queues of cars and buses waiting to cross, it was open 24 hours a day, it was relatively unaffected by the vagaries of the weather and it was faster and more reliable than had been the ferry.

However, the dogged determination of the objectors, including the famed Robbie the Pict who had established the Pictish Free State on an acre of land on Skye in 1977, won the day. In 2004 the government acquired the bridge for £27 million and abolished the tolls.

Iain, who was at the time a journalist very much involved in this tortuous but often hilarious saga, here explains what happened.

The Battle of the Bridge

Sometimes, just sometimes, the West Highlands actually lives up to all these clichés beloved of Compton Mackenzie, the Daily Record's *much mourned Ewan Bain, author of the 'Angus Og' cartoon strip, and other comical creations.*

The story of the Skye Bridge is one of those stories. As was mentioned by Rab, the bridge was the first major PFI contract (paid for by the public sector: built, at considerable profit, by the private sector) in this country. It succeeded the ferry across the Kyle Narrows, latterly a shuttle system.

It is alleged that, in the height of summer when the queues for the crossing stretched for miles, some ticket sellers were wont to ask the unsuspecting motorist: 'Fare – or bribe?' And charge accordingly. (Obviously, I can't possibly comment on these allegations.) When the last boat ran, they had a party aboard with an entire pipe band who somehow accommodated themselves on the car deck and who were joined by well-lubricated locals for a dance.

The bridge was opened on 16 October 1995 by then-Secretary of State for Scotland Michael Forsyth, a diehard Thatcherite, who entirely subscribed to the PFI notion and who enthusiastically announced that the first day's crossing would be entirely free. Afterwards, of course, the highest toll charges in Europe were due to kick in.

Having that evening reported on the day's goings-on, I retired to the lounge of the Lochalsh Hotel (orange and soda water, of course). Into the bar sashayed Robbie the Pict, who had already been campaigning against the tolls and their legality. His advice was not to leave just yet, so I didn't.

Just after midnight, in the howling dark of an October rainstorm, I stood on the Kyle end of the bridge and saw a light growing gradually in the western sky from the island side. Pipes could be heard playing. Screwing my eyes up against the sleet,

I then saw a procession of scores of protesters and island drivers coming over the new bridge and up to the toll barriers, where they refused to pay.

That pretty much set the standard for the next several years. Campaigners refused to pay the tolls and were charged by the police. Protesters staged a ceilidh dance and a picnic outing on the bridge and the constabulary were in near-permanent attendance, though relations between these hardened criminals and the cops remained remarkably amicable.

And the character of these criminals was remarkable, too. Many of those charged with refusing to pay the tolls were middle-class pillars of the establishment who would have been mortified if they'd forgotten to pay their telly licence. Among those criminally charged were several members of the new Scottish Parliament, a doctor or two, and a number of councillors. When they were called to answer these charges, the courts, in their genius, decided to hear these cases halfway across the country in Dingwall. So the protesters would cross the bridge to appear before the law and – surprise, surprise – refuse to pay the tolls, get charged again and then go on their way.

Dingwall Sheriff Court became one of the great venues for Highland journalists bent on a laugh or two: the Palladium of the North. Protesters would arrive in Dingwall, and march out to the court house, preceded by a piper or two. They would fill the court to overflowing while Sheriff James Fraser, a man of no great stature and not much humour, would sit and frown thunderously, while the prosecutor, a faintly manic fiscal called David Hingston struggled in vain to impose order, far less the fines the law demanded. Mr Hingston subsequently had a nervous breakdown, and became a defence lawyer once he'd recovered.

Frequently it all went wrong for the courts. On one occasion, Robbie the Pict – a 'known ringleader' – was slapped into jail overnight, then brought before the court the following morning under his birth name of Brian Robertson. Unfortunately, smirked Robbie, that wasn't him. He had changed his name by deed poll to Robbie the Pict some years before, so they must be after somebody else. Case dropped, judicial dignity dented and the sheriff sat smouldering on the bench like a small volcano.

On another occasion, two of the protesters – Mod gold medallist and local businessman Arthur Cormack and local councillor and postmaster Drew Millar –were locked up in Portree Police Station. A small, though non-violent riot broke out outside, constabulary reinforcements had to be called, and the two 'villains' were eventually freed.

How the tolls were eventually removed probably tells you something about the nature of our democracy. The island was represented in the Holyrood Parliament by the venerable John Farquhar Munro. He was a Liberal Democrat and his party was in a very precarious coalition with Labour. Mr Munro – whose own wife was one of those charged for non-payment – finally told the leaders of his own party that he would no longer support the coalition unless the tolls were removed.

And so in 2004, I remember standing in the shadow of the bridge in Kyle, as the First Minister Jack McConnell announced that the tolls would come off the crossing immediately. It would now be a symbol of growth and prosperity, he hoped, rather than of controversy. Drivers cheered and horns hooted as the barriers swung up, and stayed up. Justice was undoubtedly done. But I have to admit I miss the fun.

However, aside from the bridge (which is rather striking in its appearance) and the gradual intrusion of other modern means of transport, the Lochalsh region has remained much as it has been for centuries: another visually stunning Western Highland landscape of lochs, mountains, wildlife, peace and contentment.

Kyle ('Caol Loch Ailse': 'strait of the foaming loch') lies just over 60 miles to the west of Inverness. As with many other similar communities Kyle had long depended for its livelihood on fishing, crofting and dodging the excisemen. Its seclusion was rudely terminated by the appearance in 1819 of a road from Inverness, the A87, with the tourists close behind. Then, in 1897, the railway arrived, and Kyle was now firmly connected to the outside world.

The initial section of the West Highland Line from Dingwall to Stromeferry opened in 1870, but connecting it to Kyle, just a few miles to the south, took four years and 29 new bridges before the final section of track was laid at the ferry slipway beside the Lochalsh Hotel. The prediction of Kenneth MacKenzie – the 17th-century Brahan Seer – had become reality: 'The day will come when long strings of carriages without horses will run between Dingwall and Skye'. The 1963 Beeching Report almost led to the line's closure but, after a spirited campaign, it was reprieved. It was again threatened with closure in 1970, but in 1974 this decision was also reversed. Little wonder there is a museum to the Line at Kyle railway station.

Today, Kyle is an attractive village of whitewashed houses, hotels and shops, set around a natural harbour. More recent developments include a marina, salmon farm and a submarine control base. In 1980 the BBC, in its series 'Great Railway

Journeys of the World', sent Michael Palin on a journey from London to Kyle, where the ex-Monty Python man ('Nobody expects the Spanish Inquisition!') bought the Kyle of Lochalsh railway sign as an ornament for his garden.

However, as with other similar Western Highland settlements, the surrounding environment also captures the eye and the imagination. Kyle is tucked away in the southern corner of a peninsula which juts into the Inner Sound between the sea lochs of Carron and Aish, south of Loch Kishorn. A short walk west from Kyle brings you to Balmacara where the village square contains the estate's original 18th-century steadings, millhouse and icehouse. South of Kyle, across Loch Alsh and close to Glenelg, make your way to Sandaig Islands, and you'll discover where Gavin Maxwell wrote his famous book, *Ring of Bright Water*, about living with otters.

The Otter Isle

The bridge which arcs across the narrows to Skye sets down on an island in the middle of the channel. This is Eilean Ban ('white island'), where the naturalist and writer Gavin Maxwell first began his relationship with wild otters that culminated in the book and film Ring of Bright Water.

Among those who worked with Maxwell there was a teenage wildlife enthusiast called John Lister Kaye: now a baronet, Sir John Lister Kaye, a landowner, conservationist and best-selling writer. I took him back to the island and its little lighthouse just before the bridge was due to open, as part of a documentary for Radio Five Live.

John led me down to the place where the otters used to come ashore. Positioned with his back to the water, he told me enthusiastically how these feral fisher beasts used to come ashore to eat their catch.

I interrupted him at this point. 'John', I said. 'Look behind you'. Confused, he turned: to confront an otter just a few feet away, looking at him in a faintly quizzical 'should I know you?' sort of way, before giving itself a shake and plunging back into the sea. Sometimes things just happen on the West Coast.

The last turntable ferry in operation in the UK, the 'Glenachulish', runs from Glenelg across the Kylerhea straits, the shortest distance between the mainland

and Skye. The ferry has been running since 1934, despite the frequent ten-knot tides. Slightly south of Glenelg you can find the two best-preserved brochs on the Scottish mainland: Dun Telve and Dun Troddan. Finally, and you can check this out if you don't believe it, the palindromic Glenelg was officially twinned by NASA in October 2012 with a crater named Glenelg on planet Mars.

The small, pretty and today highly desirable village of Plockton, planned in the 19th century in an attempt to stem the flow of emigration from the area, is to the north of Kyle. Drumbuie, a village through which one passes on the road between Kyle and Plockton, was in the early 1970s touted as the possible site of an oil rig fabrication yard, but the plans were dropped after local and national protests, and the yard was moved to Kishorn.

House Prices and Hamish

The village of Plockton curves around a calm and peaceful bay, and palm trees dot its narrow main street, thanks to the gentle breezes of the Gulf Stream. It's described on its own website as a 'jewel' of the West Highlands. That's hard to argue with, but jewels come at a high price.

Originally called Am Ploc, it was a crofting hamlet clustered round the water until the end of the 18th century. But many of the crofters were cleared thereafter to make way for sheep farms, and the village became a port of emigration for many of those departing to the Americas.

New houses were built in Plockton, and a model village laid out. And with herring fishing booming in the 19th century, the village's population rose to around 500, with families sometimes having to live two to a cottage. This housing shortage foreshadowed what was to come in the late 20th century.

Herring, like all fish, follow their own rules. And when the migration routes changed, the herring fishing out of Plockton collapsed. After the potato famine in the 1840s, life there was so desperate it became known as 'Baile na Boichdain' – 'village of the poor'.

But Am Ploc recovered over time. One of its best ambassadors in modern times was the BBC. Or, at least, its series 'Hamish McBeth' was. It was the story of a Glasgow bobby who was transferred to some mythical, magical West Highland village. It was the breakthrough for the charismatic Scottish actor Robert Carlyle, and it was filmed in Plockton. People loved what they saw of the village, and flocked to see more. Today, its beautiful site makes it a much sought-after address. And that's brought its own problems. Try buying a house in Plockton. To be frank, you've probably got more chance in the housing hot-spot that is Edinburgh, Scotland's most expensive city.

Even at the turn of the millennium, around a third of Plockton's houses were holiday homes and therefore empty for much of the year. Americans and Europeans had joined house buyers from south of the border in driving prices beyond the reach of local youngsters, and the primary school roll was dropping at speed. Near-derelict buildings were changing hands for six-figure sums. Some ruins were bought, demolished and replaced with luxury homes that nobody lived in for much of the time. People in central London may recognise this pattern.

But there's still lots of life in Plockton, largely due to its extremely pawky and resilient population, which is refusing to give up and move on. July's Plockton Regatta is just one example, the posh-sounding name obscuring the reasonably rough-hewn and very local boating festival, which features roaring rowers representing local villages racing each other in an atmosphere of exhilaration and – er – occasional alcohol.

Calum's Seal Trips is a local company that still offers your money back if you don't see a seal on a tootle round the bay. The crofters' cattle still wander around the place, and occasionally even down the main street, though they're not supposed to. And the place has excellent hotels and restaurants for the visitor.

In recent times, Plockton also successfully fought against the loss of a major community asset. Highland Council had very sneakily proposed closing down the National Centre for Excellence in Traditional Music, based at the local school, which has produced some brilliant members of Scotland's musical community over the years. After journalists found the proposal in the small print of a cuts programme, all hell once again broke loose.

Former pupils, some of them household names, joined forces with local people and music fans across Scotland – not least top piper Dougie Pincock, principal of the centre – to fight the closure. There were mass demonstrations in Glasgow's George Square and at Highland Council headquarters and, in the end, the Council forged a compromise, and the Centre survives. If you get a chance to hear any of the pupils in action, you may think that was the right outcome. And, as a reporter who helped contribute to the campaign, so do I.

As you drive past Loch Duich westward along the A87 from Kyle you'll reach the end of the Loch near Morvich. This is close to the site of a battle in 1719 between a motley crew of Jacobites and Spaniards and the British goverment, the latter winning the day. Meanwhile, soaring above you, are the Five Sisters of Kintail.

Sisters In The Sky

The Five Sisters of Kintail are stark, dramatic peaks that thrust very high in the sky over Glen Shiel and its 'we-stock-everything' petrol station and shop: one of those truck-stop places on the road west.

This 29 square miles of estate is mostly owned by the National Trust for Scotland, and includes the Falls of Glomach, its plunging 370-feet drop making it one of Britain's highest waterfalls. 'Glomach' is Gaelic for 'gloomy'. I have only every walked the lower reaches of these hills, but I have flown over them by helicopter on a very clear day, and the ageless raw rocks, and the views from them, are stunning. If you want the names, the five mountains in question are : Sgurr na Ciste Duibhe, Sgurr na Carnach, Sgurr Fhuaran, Sgurr na Spainteach and Sgurr nan Saighead, and the entire ridge runs for about five miles. And no, none of them are called Flora or Peigi Anne, even if they are sisters. Stop being frivolous.

All of them are over 3,000 feet high, which makes them Munros, and places them among Scotland's highest mountains. Three are full Munros, while the other two are classified as subsidiary Munros, because, to use non-technical language, they sort of grow out of the others. Further east, there are three more Munros, sometimes described as The Brothers. But not by me.

Kyle of Lochalsh is at the heart of some of the most interesting and fascinating areas in the west coast of Scotland. Iain here refers again to Glenelg.

Caution

Glenelg has been mentioned. It truly is twinned with a crater on Mars, which was visited by the ill-fated Curiosity Rover in 2012. And when the twinning happened, the residents held a party in which they had a live link to NASA, and welcomed not only a US astronaut Bonnie Dunbar, the first ever to fly the space shuttle, but also the Royal Astronomer for Scotland, John C. Brown. I know, I was there.

The settlement of around 300 people runs the only regular ferry crossing to Skye, after local people managed to buy the boat and set up a community company to run it into Armadale in the beautiful Sleat Peinsula, the 'garden of Skye'. In nearby Gleann Beag, there stand two hulking Iron Age brochs, fortress-like homesteads at Dun Telve and Dun Troddan. They are buildings you can actually wander through, and wonder at. There's also the ruins of a Redcoat barracks at Bernera, built there after the first Jacobite Rising in 1715. The beach at Bernera is also worth a visit.

Glenelg is a very energetic, go-ahead community, with much to admire. But most of all, for this correspondent, is an apparently official road sign on the way into the village, the kind that normally warns of the presence of children, sheep or deer. This one refers to an even more formidable form of wildlife.

'Caution', it warns. 'Crofters on the Road'.

How can you **not** visit this most remarkable part of the Highlands?

NAIRN:

THE BRIGHTON OF SCOTLAND

Whenever I think of Nairn, which these days is admittedly not very often, my mind drifts back over half a century to the idyllic holidays I spent there in my childhood.

Every Trades Fortnight, when Inverness used to shut down for a couple of weeks in the summer, my father drove us 15 miles to our rented caravan beside Nairn's large east beach. The following two weeks were a joyful blur of playing on the beach, swimming in the chilly Moray Firth, diving off the harbour wall beside the lighthouse where the River Nairn joins the Firth, slurping ice lollies, kicking over my brother's sandcastles, throwing seaweed at dogs, and doing all the things that kids do at seaside resorts.

These were happy days, and things don't appear to have changed that much in this small resort, which sits on the eastern edge of what most people consider to be the Highlands, and where begins the flat, arable landscape of Moray, Buchan and Aberdeenshire.

I never noticed this linguistic shift as a kid, but Nairn is where the accent begins perceptibly to change from the soft, Gaelic-influenced English tongue spoken in the lands to the west of the town into a harsh, guttural, Old Scots Doric dialect which, by the time it reaches Aberdeen, is virtually incomprehensible. Examples of Doric include 'far aboots?' for 'where exactly?', 'fit like?' for 'how are you?' and 'knapdarloch' meaning 'dung hanging from knots of wool on a sheep's bottom' (there's probably an entire lexicon devoted to such as the last one: this is serious farming territory)

King David I in the 12th century, in the first of many failed attempts over the centuries to integrate the Highlands into the Scottish body politic (why do they bother?), encouraged Lowlanders to move north, and they brought with them the

'Lallans' or Old Scots dialect. These immigrants found that the area to the west of Nairn was more rugged and less fertile, had a wetter and colder climate, and was populated largely by alien Gaelic speakers. So they stayed where they were.

It has also been suggested that, to acquire more of this agriculturally productive land for themselves, these incoming Scots, along with Norman, Flemish and English settlers, 'encouraged' the original natives of Moray to relocate to the west of Nairn and into the more barren, wilder Highlands.

Over 400 years later, King James VI observed that one end of Nairn's High Street was Scots-speaking while the other end was populated by Gaels. Even today, after years of integration and assimilation, the Highland/Lowland dialect boundary begins to alter between Inverness and Nairn, and by the time one reaches Forres, the next main town along to the east, the Doric dialect and language is the accepted tongue (the 'official' border is Auldearn).

Nairn, whose name derives either from the Pictish word for 'stream' or the Gaelic for 'river of alders', is an old town of around 13,000 inhabitants (known affectionately to Invernessians as 'Nairnucks') with two long, inviting beaches, two Championship golf courses, a Telford-designed harbour, a Highland League football team, a fine view across to the Black Isle, a rich farming hinterland, and an essentially service and tourist-based economy.

Since the arrival of the railway in 1855 Nairn has been a favoured holiday destination for Lowland Scots and English tourists, including Charlie Chaplin who was a regular summer visitor, and it was described as 'The Brighton of Scotland'. It's also a town where some of those frequent visitors come to retire.

The process of invasion from the south was accelerated by the opening in 1947 of Dalcross Airport, just off the main road to Inverness, as a civil airport. Indeed, there are people today who live in Nairn, commute south from Dalcross for the working week, and return to their homes in Nairn at weekends.

Before the flood of tourists started to descend, Nairn was a spa town, although most of the local economy depended on its agricultural produce and its fishing fleet. Indeed, it was once one of northern Scotland's leading herring ports but the fleet has long since gone (as have the herring).

It's a lovely harbour, though. Highland Council is now the owner and the berths are rented to Nairn Sailing Club members.

Nairn is a town of contrasts. The west side of town was, and to a degree remains, home to the English and Scots middle- and upper-middle classes, reflected in the grand, imposing mansions, villas, luxury hotels, sandy beach and Nairn Golf Club. It is an area nostalgically evoked by David Thomson, who grew up there, in his book *Nairn in Darkness and Light*.

The centre has the air of a typical Scottish town, with its small grey-stone shops and houses and its narrow streets and, judging by my last visit, it has seen better days. Norse settlers were once thought to have occupied this area but recent scientific evidence has challenged this assertion. It was, however, the site of Nairn Castle, built in the 12th century and demolished in 1585.

Here you'll also find the grass-covered dunes, parkland and bandstand backing on to the beach and the Firth, where the Nairn Highland Games, one of Scotland's largest such Games and a major event in the town's social calendar, is held every year, normally in the middle of August.

The Havelock House, a popular, listed bar and restaurant frequented by residents of Nairn and Inverness, is to be found on Crescent Street in this part of town. The Havelock is situated opposite a house where in 2004, in one of Scotland's oddest remaining unsolved murder cases, a young Nairn banker was shot dead on his doorstep. Various explanations have been suggested, but the motive for the murder and the identity of the perpetrator remain to this day a mystery.

To the east of Nairn is Fishertown, concentrated around the River Nairn and the harbour, which was the old, working-class, fishermen area, and which fades into Nairn Dunbar Golf Club and the sand dunes and mud flats leading to Culbin Forest. This beach is wide, sandy and long, and occasionally dolphins can be spotted in the Firth. However, the further east one wanders from the harbour, the more unpredictable and potentially dangerous do the tides and sandbanks become. Both Nairn beaches were used extensively in training exercises for the D-Day Landings in World War II.

Perhaps because of Nairn's favoured location, its relative affluence, its high-end touristic appeal, its mild climate and its many natural attributes, much of the town seems to project a sense of self-satisfaction, or a cosy 'civic pride', an attitude it shares with its eastern neighbours Forres and Elgin. The rich farmlands and the sprawling, wealthy estates of the area doubtless contribute to its prosperous self-image. However, this slightly caustic observation may be revenge for my once having being hit very hard by a Nairnuck in a public house in the town.

The town lies in an area of historical interest. The Battle of Auldearn, fought in 1645 during The Wars of the Three Kingdoms, resulted in victory for the Royalists under the Marquis of Montrose over the Covenanters in Auldearn to the east of Nairn. The village took its name from the Castle of Eren built there by William the Lion in the 12th century. One of my early girlfriends lived here. Hello, Phoebe.

The night before the Battle of Culloden in 1746, where the Jacobites under Charles Edward Stuart were routed and massacred, the Hanoverian General, the Duke of Cumberland, established his 'headquarters' in Nairn. His accomodation still exists in a stone building in the grounds of Viewfield House near the Museum. His troops were encamped at nearby Balblair.

One of Scotland's most imposing tower house strongholds, Cawdor Castle, sits among splendidly laid-out gardens around five miles to the south of Nairn. The 15th-century building is owned by the Campbell family, and is best known for its supposed association with Shakespeare's Macbeth who, as 'Thane of Cawdor', died 300 years before the house was erected. This extraordinary example of mediaeval time travel could be one of the many reasons for the constant stream of visitors to the Castle.

Also in Cawdor is the Royal Brackla distillery, which was opened in 1812. It is one of the few whiskys to carry the prefix 'Royal', as King William IV was fond of it – 'the King's own whisky' – and granted it a royal warrant in 1835. It has opened and closed over the years, finally reopening in 1991. It is today run by Dewar's, who were bought by Bacardi in 1998.

Royal Brackla produces its own limited and acclaimed range of single malts, but the bulk of its malt whisky is used for blending purposes, for such as Johnny Walker's and Dewar's own brands. (Incidentally, should you ever be fortunate enough to be offered Johnny Walker Blue Label, then grab it.) Nearby are the ruins of an old RAF airfield, RAF Brackla, which was used after World War II for dismantling aircraft, mainly Halifax bombers. It closed in 1946.

In terms of evening and musical entertainment, it's fairly quiet in Nairn at present, but ask around for details. I'm sure you'll find something of interest. My abiding memory is, as a teenager, standing with around 20 or so other kids and watching supergroup Cream in 1967 in the legendary Ballerina Ballroom who also put on legendary bands like Pink Floyd and The Who, as well as loads of impressive local bands.

The Ballerina occupied what was once Nairn Public Hall, built in the 1870s. Since the Ballroom's demise as a dance hall, it has been a clothing shop and a bingo hall and, in 2008, local resident and actress Tilda Swinton staged a quirky film festival, 'The Ballerina Ballroom Theatre of Dreams'. When I last passed by, the building was empty.

The Outsider

Tilda Swinton, Oscar-winning actor, is a long-term resident of Nairn. So that meant her husband also lived there. Her husband (now ex-husband) is one of Scotland's most talented and eccentric individuals: the artist and writer John Byrne.

As a writer he produced the 'Slab Boys' trilogy for the stage, and wrote the hugely successful 'Tutti Frutti' for the telly, the series which really launched Robbie Coltrane, Emma Thompson and Richard Wilson (that may be Victor Meldrew to you).

Graduating as a painter from Glasgow School of Art, he is probably by now one of Scotland's most successful and certainly individual artists, exhibited everywhere and most recently at the Scottish National Portrait Gallery where his show was entitled 'Sitting Ducks'. His paintings are often moody, sometimes surreal and always intense. He's an outsider but one who has succeeded on his own terms.

He has never had any difficulty in expressing himself. When his alma mater Glasgow School of Art burned down in 2015, John Byrne, appearing in a public session in Inverness, didn't say 'served 'em right'. What he did ask was what people were doing with aerosols in an art school.

And when I went to see him to do an interview on something the entire time was so diverting I can't even remember what the original subject was. His particular bête noir *was the newly instituted Scottish smoking ban, which he had just come across for the first time, and of which he most certainly didn't approve. Mind you, on the same occasion, I also got a private viewing of his drawings for the original 'Tutti Frutti' characters, which bear a startling resemblance to the stuff he's been producing most recently, harking back to his youth in Paisley, in the Teddy Boy era.*

John Byrne no longer lives in Nairn which, from my point of view, is a great pity. He definitely illuminated Highland life.

The town's local history and culture can be accessed at the Museum, originally established in 1858 and now to be found at Viewfield House, and the Community and Arts Centre offers a busy programme of film, arts and music, as well as the Book and Art Festival every June. The Little Theatre in Fishertown, set up in 1946, is particularly popular for its Christmas panto, among other events.

The local football team is Nairn County, founded in 1914 and a member of the Highland League. Although they generally do fairly well in the League, they have managed to win the title only once (1976) in their history.

Champion-ees

Nairn County remains a force in the Highland League. They have not won it a lot, though. However, back in 1976, they were taken in hand by one of the great unsung managers of north football, teacher Innes McDonald.

The team he assembled was a squad of honest, workmanlike players with probably more skill than most people gave them credit for, a mixture on the lines of the classic non-league cup tie team: delivery men, teachers, even a policeman who proceeded in a south-easterly direction to score a load of goals up front. Slowly, it began to dawn on the rest of the Highland League power brokers that the wee County were going to win something. And this gave other teams a problem.

That was as nothing to the problem it gave Nairn fans. Unaccustomed as they were to such success, they spent part of the season deliberating on what their chant should be. They'd never really needed one before. But, finally, a masterstroke. Think back to the great Dave Dee, Dozy, Beaky, Mick and Titch, those giants of 1960s pop. Remember their great 'Hold Tight'?. Then hear the full glory of the Nairn Chant, as they rampaged to the title. It goes like this:

'Clap-clap. Clap-clap-clap. Clap-clap-clap-clap. Nern-Nern.'
Genius, pure genius.

The town's two championship golf clubs are Nairn Dunbar (at the back of my old caravan site near Fishertown), which is Scottish Golf Club of the Year in 1915, and Nairn Golf Club, on the upmarket west side of town, which has hosted the Curtis Cup and the Walker Cup as well as all the main British and European Amateur Championships. It is normally seen as 'posher' than Dunbar, although in my experience the latter is a more difficult course.

As we mentioned earlier, the east beach between Dunbar and the sea is a wide expanse of dunes and sand which, if you're a kid, appears to stretch for ever. In fact, it merges into Culbin Sands which after a few miles arrives at Findhorn Bay. The tides can be fast-moving and potentially treacherous around here.

Indeed, in the mid-20th century a family of eight became confused by the mist and the rapidly encroaching tidal channel, and they were drowned just a couple of miles along the beach. Today's safety measures have much improved the situation but it'll do no harm to keep your eyes open.

One final thing: the name of the place is pronounced 'Nern' and not 'Nayrn'. Remember this when you visit, as you should do. It's a pleasant, diverting little place and yet another illustration of the splendid variety of the Highland region. But only just.

PORTREE:

THE MISTY ISLE

'A man came ridin' oot the west one wild and stormy day
He was quiet, lean, and hungry – his eyes were smokey grey
He was lean across the hurdies, but his shooders they were big
The terror o' the heilan' glens – that was the Portree Kid'

So begins a ballad – 'The Portree Kid' – which was performed by Scottish folk duo The Corries.

It's an entertaining, tongue-in-cheek song, although a po-faced listener could interpret it as patronising and would probably prefer the twee cosiness of the 'Skye Boat Song' ('Speed. bonny boat, like a bird on the wing...'). However, I find the lyrics an affectionate recognition of the inhabitants of Portree, the largest and liveliest settlement on the Isle of Skye.

With its buildings clustered round an attractive natural harbour fringed by hills and cliffs, the town of Portree lies on the east coast of Skye. It is known in Gaelic as 'Port Righ' ('the king's port'), which refers to a visit by King James V in 1540 in an attempt to secure the support of the Western Isles clans, although an earlier name for the town was the similar-sounding 'Port Ruigeadh' ('slope harbour'). Prior to the 16th century, it was called 'Kiltaraglen': 'the Church of St Talarican' ('Cill Targhiain'). Today, around a third of the 2,500 inhabitants are Gaelic speakers.

Hold The Front Page

Skye has its own local media, as has many another community across the Highlands and Islands. The BBC has a presence in Portree, its studio which contributes to Gaelic television and radio programmes like Aithris na Maidne on Radio nan Gaidheal, and An La on BBC Alba television, is situated rather strangely above a local bank.

But perhaps its best known media presence is not in Portree, but down the road in the busy little village of Broadford: the West Highland Free Press *launched in 1971, originally in a big house at the head of the ferry pier at Kyleakin. Back then, there was a team of four former Dundee University students, led by editor Brian Wilson, who had decided to launch a left-leaning paper in an area they thought was in need of a radical publication.*

They were initially an enterprise somewhere between a commune and a co-operative, paying themselves a flat-rate weekly wage of just ten pounds. From the start, they were less than gentlemanly, branding their nearest competitor, the Stornoway Gazette *the 'Stornoway Greysheet', and launching an early wide-screen campaign against a plan to use Drumbuie on the mainland as the site of a major oil construction yard. They won that campaign, and the* Free Press *had truly arrived in the West Highlands.*

There is somewhere in BBC Scotland's archives a television programme which features a young and rather hairy Brian Wilson confronting the chief of the Clan Donald, Lord Godfrey Macdonald, in the bar at Kinloch Lodge, which the Macdonalds owned and from which Lady Clare Macdonald – of cookery book and column fame – still operates. It was a very interesting nose-to-nose, and a particular corrective to the forelock-tugging school of most journalists in the Highlands back then.

At that time, I used sometimes to provide a probably not very savoury bed but not breakfast – look, we were all very young – for whichever member of staff came to Inverness to oversee the printing of that week's paper. I also occasionally travelled over to Skye to help out with the 'stuffing' of the paper: putting the pages in order, ready for the newsagents.

I can testify to the excitement the Free Press *brought to Skye and beyond – a campaigning paper in tune, particularly, with many of the younger demographic in the West Highlands. The paper went from strength to strength, campaigning on issues like the land and the Gaelic language, and establishing itself as an outstanding addition to the range of local newspapers in the north. As well as Brian Wilson, columnists of quality have included the Gaelic writer Angus Peter Campbell, Professor Donald Macleod, who was the principal of the Free Church College, the writer Roger Hutchinson and the incomparable 'View From North Lochs', a surreal saunter through the mind of the late and much-lamented Aimsir Eachainn.*

The newspaper has gone on to win many press prizes over the years, including Highlands and Islands Newspaper of the Year. *By any measurement, it has fulfilled the ambitions of those young former students from back in the 1970s. Brian Wilson went on to a highly successful political career, becoming a UK government minister and setting in place schemes designed to help the very communities 'at the edge', to which he had brought a newspaper.*

He is no longer an editor though, or indeed a columnist, with the now employee-owned Free Press. *In 2015, Professor Macleod wrote a column about Islam in the UK. He was asked to 'moderate his language' by the editor, refused and resigned. Brian Wilson wrote a column in the newspaper defending Professor Macleod's right to freedom of speech. He was sacked for 'breach of trust': though the paper actually printed the column. At the time of writing, there seems little likelihood of this row healing over. Brian Wilson is now a major figure in the revival of the Harris Tweed industry and an occasional columnist for some national newspapers. The* Free Press *soldiers on.*

In the late 18th century, the island's escalating poverty and overpopulation persuaded hundreds of Portree dwellers to ship themselves off to America and Canada in the hope of bettering their condition. James Boswell, in *Journal of a Tour to the Hebrides*, remarked in 1773; 'the people on shore were almost distracted when they saw their relations go off... they seemed to think they would soon follow'. However, the local laird, Sir James MacDonald, arrested this population decline by developing Portree into a commercially successful fishing port, thereby producing much-needed employment.

In 1821 steamships began regular trips to Tarbert and Kyleakin, where the ferry crossed to the mainland, and in 1851 the weekly steamer from Glasgow to Stornoway began to stop at Portree. Meanwhile, Thomas Telford in the 1820s built roads linking Portree with Kyleakin and with Uig to the north, and he also constructed the pier on Portree harbour. By 1894, there was a daily steamer to Strome Ferry, Ullapool, Oban, Lochinver and other towns up and down the West Coast.

During the winter of 1846/47, the Potato Famine caused extreme hardship throughout the Western Highlands, and Portree was no exception to its ravages. Various organisations, including the Free Church of Scotland, tried their utmost to alleviate this desperate situation, and an Englishman who rejoiced under the splendid name of Sir Edward Pine Coffin commandeered British Navy ships to distribute oatmeal from storage depots which he established at Tobermory and Portree. This admirable gentleman deserves to be better remembered for his humanitarian deeds during the crisis, as does the Free Church, to whom the religious affiliation of the sufferers was of no importance in their efforts.

Portree, and Skye generally, suffered from The Clearances, but a few people living near Portree played a crucial role in helping to bring to an end this devastating expropriation of crofting lands in the Highlands. In 1881, in the village of Camastianavaig a few miles south of Portree, a number of crofters faced eviction but they refused to move their sheep or pay the rent due to the landlord, Lord MacDonald. They also forced the terrified Sheriff's Officer to burn their eviction notices in front of them.

In early 1882, 50 policemen arrived from Glasgow to attempt to enforce the eviction orders, but the police raid was unexpectedly counter-attacked by crofters, comprised of around 100 men, women and children armed only with sticks, stones and a good deal of courage. As the chorus of the song 'The Battle of the Braes' has it:

'Oh the battle was long but the people were strong
You shoulda been there that day'.

This was a critical turning point in The Clearances. The crofters' anger spread across the island and into the mainland. The 'Battle of the Braes' led to the formation of the Highland Land League, with the police and landlords' tactics arousing outrage far beyond Skye and the Highlands.

The government came under strong pressure to launch an enquiry, and they set up the Napier Commission. The Commission's findings led to the passing of the 1886 Crofters Act, granting legal security of tenure and the right of inheritance to crofters. The Crofters Commission, a government body, was established to protect and defend crofters' rights, and in time The Clearances withered away, although the shells of many deserted cottages remain.

Today, Portree harbour is teeming with fishing boats and pleasure craft, while the houses around the harbour are a mixture of brightly painted and natural stone and whitewashed buildings. On the southern peninsula of the harbour is an area of land known as 'The Lump', which was once the forum for public hangings. The town's main street is Bank Street, on which stands the Royal Hotel on the site of the old McNab's Inn, where Prince Charlie bade his final farewell to Flora MacDonald in 1746.

Portree, and Skye generally, is an interesting mixture of social classes, from fishermen to landed aristocrats. The Skye Gathering Hall can be found in the town, and it hosts, unsurprisingly, the annual Skye Gathering Ball, which is an annual riotous social event for the wealthier landed inhabitants of the island. In 2008, the Ball got out of hand, leading to the *Daily Record* headline: 'Posh ball mayhem as gatecrasher headbutts laird's son', a headline which would be difficult to invent.

'Who's Got The Cup?'

Football is played on Skye. In fact, there's a flourishing West Highland League which features teams from the island. But really, the game on Skye is shinty, which has variously been described as 'hockey with violence' and 'a riot with a ball and clubs'.

It is similar to hockey, in that the game is played with clubs, known as 'camans', and a ball, but players are allowed to play the ball in the air and with either face of the caman. It's extremely physical and very fast, is played on a pitch of more than 140 yards' length and teams of twelve shooting into a small goal, similar in construction to an ice hockey cage, but taller. It can get bloody.

The game was played in Scotland before records began. By the late 19th century, however, teams from Portree and Bernisdale were succeeded by Skye Camanachd. In the 1960s, the club all but foundered, as other clubs tried to force the islanders to play all their games on the mainland.

Skye Camanachd was reconstituted in 1969, with one of the island's great characters, Colonel Jock Macdonald, joining forces with police inspector Duncan MacIntyre to relaunch the club. In 1990, Skye finally won the 'Scottish Cup of shinty', the game's top prize, the Camanachd Cup, for the first time ever. At the heart of the team was another great of the game, D.R. Macdonald, who had coached many of the players at Portree High School, where he was a Gaelic teacher. Managed by Ross Cowie, Skye beat one of the game's greatest clubs, Newtonmore, at Fort William. The island hardly turned a hair – well, except for the 5,000 people, around half Skye's population, who turned up in Portree's main square to greet the returning heroes.

You can very easily find someone in Portree who will enthusiastically recall that great and golden season. The entire thing was filmed for a BBC television programme called 'Home', directed by Skye native Douglas Mackinnon who has gone on to award-winning fame directing programmes such as 'Sherlock' and 'Doctor Who'.

What the film documented was a great day in island history. We perhaps should draw a veil over what followed: Portree's party to end all parties. It culminated at a fairly late hour of the following morning with the extremely expensive trophy being found all alone on a Portree street, not so very far from the team's unofficial headquarters, the Tongadale bar, on Wentworth Street.

Everybody thought somebody else was looking after it, it's claimed. On the other hand, the trophy may well have beaten a retreat from the awful prospect of being in a small room with a team of hairy-arsed, celebrating shinty players and their followers. It may be safe now.

Portree is home to Skye's only secondary school, Portree High. I recall one very wet day playing football against them, when I was at Inverness Royal Academy, on their pitch in the town, and I can testify to the friendship and hospitality they showed us (even after we beat them).

Culturally, Portree is an interesting town. The Aros Heritage Centre, with its panoramic views on the southern edge of the town, offers a visitor centre, theatre, cinema, art shows, exhibitions on the history of the town and the island and storytelling, and the visitor can even watch a sea-eagle's nest live on CCTV. There is also a vibrant and exciting music scene, with a strong emphasis on contemporary folk music, in Portree and across Skye.

The island of Raasay (from the Norse for 'Isle of the roe deer') separates Skye from the mainland and is only about three miles (by sea) from Portree. It's an intriguing island, historically and geologically. It's the birthplace of the Scottish Renaissance poet Sorley MacLean, and the composer Harrison Birtwistle was a resident here for several years. However, the less-heralded Calum MacLeod, a crofter and lighthouse keeper at Arnish to the north of the island, is remembered more than anyone for his persistence and determination on behalf of his fellow islanders.

After fruitless years of trying to persuade the local council to build a road on the island, he spent ten years between 1964 and 1974 building it himself. Armed only with basic hand tools and a wheelbarrow, Calum built a two-mile road – known today as 'Calum's Road' – between Arnish and the ruins of the 15th-century Brochel Castle. He can be regarded as a true local hero. A cairn by the roadside commemorates his Herculean undertaking. Songs have been written and stage and radio plays have been performed about this man, who died in 1988 but whose memory lingers on.

The Isle of Raasay

The island of Raasay was visited, on their peregrinations, by Dr Johnson and Mr Boswell in 1773, where they dined with Macleod of Raasay and Dr Johnson boasted of having crossed the Atlantic in an open boat.

Raasay has certainly made its mark on Highland history. After the Macleods ran out of money, and emigrated to Australia in 1843, it was sold to a series of landlords, who methodically cleared the place. One such landlord, George Rainy, built a wall across the island, from one coast to the other, to separate the remaining people in the north of the island from his sheep in the south.

Hundreds of people were cleared, and some townships simply disappeared. In the 20th century, land raiders took back parts of the island, and eventually, despite jail terms, won the land back. But by the 1960s, another absentee laird took control of Raasay.

Dr John Green was sold the island for a knock-down price, and even then took many years to complete the purchase. He then set about vetoing any possible improvements to the island he'd bought but hardly ever visited, and never stayed on overnight. He opposed even a ferry link to neighbouring Skye and became notorious as 'Dr No', coinciding with the publication of that James Bond book. Eventually the Highlands and Islands Development Board was persuaded to buy the laird out, though only after something like 20 years. Things got a great deal better after that, though depopulation, especially of the north end, continued apace. Young people left the place to go to school, and tended not to return, seeking their living elsewhere.

West Highland Free Press *writer Roger Hutchinson wrote* Calum's Road: *'there alone, in an empty landscape, he began to build a road'. Calum Macleod built Calum's Road because of that depopulation at the north end. It was, as observed elsewhere, a remarkable and somewhat bloody-minded achievement, and as he built, Calum at one point smashed through Rainy's Wall and left only stony fragments of that icon of feudalism. But the road didn't really stem the population drift.*

So you might have thought when the chance came to lead the land reform campaign, the remaining crofters of Raasay would have snatched at it. In 1989, Lord Sanderson of Bowden, then a minister in the Scottish Office, offered the crofters of Raasay the chance to take over their own land. Things had improved so much under the aegis of the government's Department of Agriculture and Fisheries for Scotland (DAFS), however, that the crofters of Raasay said thanks. But no thanks.

There was one benefit of this non-event that may not have been immediately evident. A Stornoway-based lawyer called Simon Fraser worked on the legal problems involved with transferring the crofts to the community. Though this one didn't happen, he garnered enough experience and expertise in the byzantine byways of crofting law that he went on to advise the Assynt Crofters, when they took control of their land, and provided vital advice to many communities that were to follow Assynt's lead. When he died in 2016, he was rightly garlanded in praise by these same communities.

Some may have regretted that they had turned down control when in 2013, the Scottish government sold the crofters' sporting rights on a lease to an Ayrshire game stalking company. The crofters on the island accused the SNP government of acting like an absentee landlord, and ministers eventually backtracked, awarding the rights to the crofters for five years with a further five-year option.

Raasay House, where Johnson and Boswell were entertained, has also had its own chequered history. Dr Green's former residence housed an adventure school and then the Raasay Outdoor Centre in modern times. It was purchased by a community company who set about a multimillion pound programme to restore it, only for a major fire to all but gut the building in 2007, just weeks before the job was due to end.

The work was re-tendered and won by a Highland company, ROK, who set about rebuilding the place. Then in 2010, ROK collapsed and the house was once more in limbo. But new contractors were found and in 2013, Raasay House reopened. It's now a popular café and hotel. It's never quiet for long on Raasay.

Back in Portree, if you're in search of a challenging, physical experience you should visit the Totternish Ridge, to the north of the town, which is composed of dramatic rock formations formed by a series of land slips. These formations include the Old Man Of Storr, the Kilt Rock and the bizarre pinnacles of the Quiraing, the rocks of which are still in process of geological movement. The word 'Quiraing' (in Gaelic 'Cuith-Raing') derives from the Old Norse for a 'round fold'. This is one of the several places on the island where the old Gaelic inhabitants used to hide their cattle from Viking raiders.

The Cuillin ('black') Hills to the south of Portree are moody, unpredictable and world-famous among hill walkers and climbers, but you need to know what you're doing before you venture on to the Black Mountains or you could cause damage to yourself and others. However, if you're a competent or skilled climber the views from the Cuillins are stunning.

Down the Gaelic Motorway

Skye is famed – rightly – for its fantastic scenery. And some of the most spectacular is to be found to the south of the island. The district of Sleat is branded 'the Garden of Skye', lush and green and very different in character from the rugged high lands of the north of the island.

It also has a road. The route left from the main Portree road will take you in the direction of Armadale to the south of the peninsula, passing on its way one of the most spectacular sites boasted by any place of further education in the country.

Looking out over the sea, Sabhal Mor Ostaig (it translates as 'the big barn at Ostaig') is Scotland's Gaelic college and a hub of the University of the Highlands and Islands. It started serious teaching in, and about, the Gaelic languagein the 1970s-1980s. Today it is officially the National Centre for Gaelic Language and Culture, teaching Gaelic broadcasting and multi-media, business management and IT, as well as music, literature, media studies, language planning and economic development.

There are 84 study bedrooms on site, and the college also does distance learning. Such is its popularity (not to mention the political skills of those involved with it) that the exceptionally good road down to the college is known locally as the Gaelic Motorway.

And the college puts itself about internationally. Recently, its website was blandly noting that recent visitors had included 'Madame Tan Xiutan from the Chinese Embassy, Danny Alexander (then a Highland MP and Chief Secretary to the Treasury) and our old friends, the Sami (they might once have been called Eskimos)'. The brackets, by the way, are mine. You too can visit. They conduct tours of the spectacular college buildings, if you phone ahead.

STORNOWAY:
CAPITAL OF THE OUTER HEBRIDES

A 'cheuchter', the vulgar and more common spelling of the Gaelic 'teuchter', is defined in the *Urban Slang Online Dictionary* as follows: 'any Highland man who likes nothing better than a good fecht (fight) with his house, after a gallon of whisky and then into bed for a frolic with his beloved sheep wife'.

This is clearly an insulting opinion aired by a Scots Lowlander to describe Highlanders, who even in the late 19th century were regarded by many southern Scots (for whom the Gaels originally coined the word 'sassenachs') as a feckless, idle and genetically inferior race. Perhaps these Lowlanders should look in a mirror?

However, in my Highland hometown of Inverness the word 'cheuchter' is an affectionate, if mildly teasing, word used to describe someone who originates from further north-west in the Highlands than does the teaser. In this context, it would be difficult to find anyone more of a 'cheuchter' (or, more endearingly, a 'coast-wester') than a native of Stornoway, one of the furthest north-west towns in the British Isles. With a population of approximately 9,000 'cheuchters' (sorry, 'inhabitants'), this is a natural, sheltered port on the east coast of the Isle of Lewis in the Outer Hebrides and is, by some degree, the largest settlement in the Western Isles.

The Long Island

This may seem like a petite divertissement, *but it is about language. I start my treatise on Stornoway, and its surrounding land mass, in Aberdeen.*

As a callow and newly-arrived youth in the Granite City, I was greeted by someone I didn't know with the ringing cry: 'Fit like, loon?' My first instinct was to engage in some non-verbal violence on the grounds that a) I didn't understand a word of that, and b) it sounded very much as if I was being accused of having certain mental issues. In fact, he was merely enquiring after my health... and 'loon' doesn't mean what I thought it meant.

I should have known better, as I had done my growing-up in a place that also had its own indigenous language. In Aberdeen and much of the north-east, theirs goes by the name of Doric. In Stornoway, I'm not quite sure what it is. It is neither English nor Gaelic, but it is unique to the alleged capital of the Western Isles. So, in a spirit of helpfulness, here is just a very short sample. In Stornoway, you're not a bloke, a laddie, or even a manny. The correct term here is 'cove'. Yes: cove. If you inhabit the distaff side, on the other hand, you may be called many things, particularly by a Stornoway male, but what you are properly is a 'blone'.

Stornoway is my native heath. Therefore, I'm biased. As a youth, I couldn't wait to get away from the place. Now, I seem to be back there frequently. That, in the past, has been Stornoway's problem. Not getting rid of me (that would count as a plus for most communities). But traditionally, Stornoway youngsters got an education at my alma mater, the Nicholson Institute, in order to go away, first to university or college, and then frequently to a working life on the mainland or further afield.

Even if not bound for the Groves of Academe, many Stornowegians might go to Glasgow, Aberdeen or elsewhere to start careers in nursing, for example, or the police. (Indeed it's reckoned Glasgow still boasts the largest Gaelic-speaking population in Scotland, at somewhere over 5,000 claiming to speak the language.) Some of this still happens but, even in this Age of Austerity, things have changed in Stornoway.

As a junior football goalkeeper, the pitch where I made one of my finest saves that helped to put us into a cup final (in which we were subsequently tanned, and I was awful) is now a supermarket. (Sadly, the cup final venue is still with us.) The cinema which was allegedly cursed by a succession of Free Church ministers for screening the Biblical epic 'The Greatest Story Ever Told' is also no longer with us, but not because of a curse, in my non-superstitious submission. Woolworths, of course, where generations of island teens learned how to shoplift, has also closed.

But some things remain. One of Stornoway's great features for the outdoor-minded is the Castle Grounds, part of the legacy of Leverhulme mentioned by Rab a bit later in this article. The Grounds surround Lews Castle, which in my youth was a college teaching various technical subjects, foremost among them the art and science of navigation to generations of sailors.

The Grounds roll on forever, some of them landscaped, some of them not, but these days lots of them stripped off the massed rhodedendrons, which were a delight to the eye but were gradually poisoning the soil beneath.. Still, the Castle Grounds offer various delightful walks, like the one out to Cuddy Point, where many of Stornoway's youth used to gather to swim and party in the days before the place had a swimming pool: though perhaps not like the one we young people used to indulge in, which went by the name of 'bushwalking'. It entailed walking on top of the bushes all the way to the wide empty spaces of the Barvas Moor, outside of Stornoway, without touching the ground. I have no idea why.

These days, the Grounds play host to the big tent that is the centrepiece of the annual Heb Celt Music festival, an event that is growing in scope and importance every year, attracting an audience from across Scotland and much further afield and artists equally far scattered and far more famous. I watched Van Morrison live in the Castle Grounds a few years ago: an experience I could never have dreamed of, growing up there in the 1960s.

It was also in the Castle Grounds that I met the first world champion boxer I'd ever come across, while we were both peeing on a tree. This episode of mutual micturating was no more than that, so don't get the wrong idea. They didn't have that sort of stuff when I was a youth in Stornoway. His name was Walter McGowan. He was the flyweight champion of the world, in an era when there only was one world title: he was from Hamilton, he became the first Scottish world champion boxer to be made an MBE, and he was a very nice guy. He died during the writing of this book.

He was in Stornoway as guest of honour at the town's faintly insane Carnival, which otherwise involves many foolish floats, music and drinking, all of which Stornoway does very well. My other overpowering memory of the Carnival is being refused an autograph by the Rangers and Scotland winger Billy Henderson, when a posse of Rangers players were the celebs of that summer. It wasn't entirely unreasonable, as I had neither paper nor pen on me at the time.

If the Carnival attracted many famous names to Stornoway, then Stornoway and the surrounding island didn't do badly at breeding its own. One of the finest singers ever to come out of the islands, Calum Kennedy, came from Lewis and was a pupil at the Nicolson Institute a few years ahead of me. I am in no position to pronounce on the truth of the claim that he was expelled for booting an unloved female teacher up the behind, but it's a story I've been told many times. He certainly applied a similar kick to Gaelic music in subsequent years and the dynasty he created has continued that tradition.

While we're on my alma mater, let's hear it for the team of brainboxes who won the BBC's nationwide inter-school competition 'Top of the Form' in the 1960s, when just getting off the island was an epic achievement (when our family went anywhere, our car was swept up into a cargo net and swung on board the steamer).

Let's hear it for an art teacher called Donny B. Macleod who became one of the best known names on nation-wide television in the 1970s, presenting programmes like 'Nationwide' and 'Pebble Mill At One', before dying young, at the age of 52.

Let's hear it for Iain Crichton Smith, who wrote some of Scotland's finest 20th Century literature in his second language (that would be English), and the Gaelic poet Derick Thomson, who came from the same village.

In the modern era, let's hear it too for wizards of the word like Kevin Macneil, who produced in The Stornoway Way *one of the finest, most nihilistic descriptions of dead-end youth trying to grow up in a remote island community, a story which could have been set in many an urban slum. Let me put it this way. If he'd been born in Edinburgh, you'd never have heard of Irvine Welsh, but the Tourist Board probably wouldn't want to hire him. Though he did also write* Love And Zen In The Outer Hebrides.

However, I'm assuming you are a tourist and want to know about Tourist Stuff. Stornoway has no shortage of bars, from the modern and genteel to, er, the Star Inn. This latter is best referred to as 'atmospheric', but, as in many of Stornoway's licensed premises, you'll get a conversation should you seek one, sometimes on frankly surreal subjects.

There are not, it must, be admitted, large numbers of fine dining establishments, but I would recommend Digby Chick's. Also, the last time I ate there, the restaurant at the An Lantair Museum was not to be sniffed at. In these entirely subjective peregrinations, I would recommend a trip or two out of town: whether that's to the golden beaches and dramatic seascapes of Uig; to the watery delights of Lochs, which does what it says on that tin; or to the Far North where the Niseachs live.

Ness is a little kingdom all of its own. The natives are Niseachs, and they have what might be described as an undue conceit of themselves. This is not without some justification, as they have produced some great Gaelic scholars, creative people across all of the arts, are hard-headed horse traders in the matter of high finance and also pretty good at football. Ness are past winners of the Highland Amateur Cup.

But their diet leaves a lot to be desired. The Ness specialty is the 'guga'. It's the young of the solan goose, which nest in vast numbers on the rock called Sula Sgeir, forty miles north of Lewis. Every year, a team of men from Ness is chosen to sail north to the rock, to scale it, slaughter thousands of the birds, and bring them back, to great celebration.

The first recorded mention of the guga hunt was by Dean Munro in 1549, though it may well have been going on before that. The birds are caught with nooses round the neck and killed with a blow to the head. The hunters stay in stone bothies on the rock for a couple of weeks. Once the food of Scottish kings, it is still considered a delicacy in Ness today.

Brown paper parcels of dead guga are sent round the world to Ness exiles, to their great excitement and subsequent delight. So maybe you should take their word for how good it is. Myself – and I have lived at addresses where the guga arrived by mail – I would advise against even trying a delicacy that smells like diesel and tastes like fish. Or, that may be the other way round.

Finally, for further ramblings, may I suggest heading south. The other half of the island of Lewis is quaintly known as the Isle of Harris, for all that it is well and truly welded to the bigger, richer half. Until the 1970s, and the advent of the first Island Council, it was actually in a different county. It boasts absolutely stunning beaches: the one at Luskentyre seems to go on forever, and on a sunny day, the shimmer makes it impossible to see to the end of it.

It has 'coffin roads', which were used by communities cleared from the fertile west coast to the rocky moonscape on the other side, to transport their dead back to a place where you could actually get a spade into the ground.

You can't go wandering in Harris, though, without reference to The Big Cloth ('clo-mhor'). As a youth, I used to read in a rather staid comic called the Eagle about the exploits of a detective called Harris Tweed. Somehow, even in next-door Lewis, I never really understood the connection, probably because the detective seemed to have more in common with the Home Counties than with the weaver's shed down the road. But this is the real home of Harris Tweed, which is now very heavy duty cloth indeed. It's no thanks to Haggas, some will tell you. But first, here's the history.

Harris Tweed begins with the wool of Hebridean sheep which is processed – traditionally by soaking it in urine – then woven into cloth by weavers all over the Long Island, before being made up into clothing at one of the island's tweed mills.

The Countess of Dunmore began the modern story in 1846. As a landowner in Harris, she commissioned two sisters from the village of Strond – known as the Paisley Sisters, because they'd trained there as weavers – to weave lengths of tweed, and had them made up as jackets for her gamekeepers and ghillies. She then promoted this weatherproof clothing to fellow estate owners for their staff, for themselves and for their huntin' shootin' and fishin' guests. In just a few years, it became the fashionable choice in Victorian court circles.

Harris Tweed prospered. It was identified by the trade mark Orb, which only appears on the genuine product. It's protected by law. So everything looked rosy in the 20th century. Then, demand began to drop off. The trouble is Harris Tweed is so hard-wearing that, once a chap's bought a jacket, it's likely to last him all his life and he may never buy another. And in the modern market place, Harris Tweed became wholly identified with customers of a certain age and style, just like that Eagle detective.

As the industry became becalmed, enter Brian Haggas. The Yorkshire businessman, who had worked in textiles all his life, acquired the island's biggest tweed mill in 2006, and announced that he was cutting the number of patterns from thousands to just four – and he'd only be making gents' jackets. The weavers were not impressed.

Enter then Brian Wilson, the retired government minister whom we last met as the young editor of the West Highland Free Press in Skye. He and a consortium, backed by a retired oil executive among others, bought a disused tweed mill in Shawbost on the West Side of Lewis. Harris Tweed Hebrides offered the weavers an alternative market, and within a few years controlled around 90 per cent of all output. Harris Tweed became fashionable all over again, and new, lighter cloth was modelled on catwalks the world over. Harris Tweed Hebrides won fashion trophies and export awards.

Now there are more weavers than ever before, and some of them you can visit. There's Donald John Mackay at Luskentyre, for instance. He is the very epitome of The Cloth's recovery, making headlines when sports shoe manufacturers Nike ordered 9,000 metres of his cloth to add trim to their shoes.

There are other retail outlets in Tarbert, Plockrapool, Grosebay and Drinishader. At some of these, you can watch a weaver at work, but be warned. The roads of Harris are not exactly three-lane motorways, so you will require a sense of adventure on your journey of discovery. It's also only fair to say that there are probably more weavers and outlets in Lewis than in Harris. But this is the home of the Big Cloth. Have a look.

It would be remiss of me, even if you're on a flying visit to Harris, not to recommend Seallam, which is a historical centre, genealogical research base and shop at Northton, on your way south from the capital, Tarbert. It's presided over by Bill Lawson, who's originally from Stirling but who has made Harris his home. Along with his wife Chris, he has set up a place specialising in island history and where you can look up your own family tree, if it touches on the islands.

Here you can pick up and hold pottery which was first handled 2,000 years ago (that's spooky), wander round the exhibitions that chart the story of the islands through the ages, and peruse loads of books specialising in island subjects. And here, as well as in other places, you'll find stunning photographs for sale, notably those of one John Maher, a resident of Leverburgh ('an t-Obbe') and once the drummer with Buzzcocks. His long-exposure portraits of island artefacts and icons will make you look twice. That's a promise.

Back on the sight-seeing trail, St Clement's Church in Rodel, at the south end, is a 16th-century church that features the magnificent tomb of Alasdair Crotach, lying in state at your feet. And while you're there, there is the Rodel Hotel, a fine watering hole and seafood eatery for locals, tourists and the many yachties, who cluster off the south end in the summer. None of these should be missed.

D'you think they'll let me back in?

Although there have been settlements in this area since at least 6,000 BC, the Vikings founded the town in the 9th century AD, naming it 'Stjornavagr' ('steering bay'). Its Gaelic name is 'Steornabhagh'. After the departure of the Norsemen in the 13th century, the Nicholson family, of Norse descent, took over the running of Stornoway and Lewis. Their name lives on today in the Nicholson Institute, mentioned by Iain and which is the secondary school in Stornoway.

The Clan MacLeod – known locally as 'Siol Torquil', Gaelic for 'Torquil's seed' – then became the landowners until 1506 when the Earl of Huntly captured Stornoway Castle. In 1598 the fiercely independent townspeople resisted attempts by King James VI to incorporate the town into a formal trading agreement with mainland Scotland, and his attempted importation onto the island of Dutch settlers and sassenachs from Fife was unsuccessful.

In 1610 the MacKenzies of Seaforth acquired the island and, despite the strenuous efforts of Oliver Cromwell half a century later to occupy Stornoway, they retained overlordship until they sold it in 1844 to one James Matheson, who had made his fortune in the Chinese opium trade, so he was clearly a man of high ethical and moral principles.

In 1918 Matheson sold it on to William Lever, 1st Viscount of Leverhulme, whose ambitious plans for expansion of the island's economy were met with local scepticism by many locals who held different opinions on the town's future. So in 1923, in a remarkable gesture, Lever created the Stornoway Trust to administer the town and he effectively gave the land back to the people. The establishment of the Trust is regarded as a landmark victory for the common people in the history of land use in Scotland.

Maws and Townies

In 1975, local government reorganisation in Scotland meant that the islands had their own council running their affairs from its Stornoway headquarters for the first time in the modern era. That meant new white-collar jobs running all those services that local authorities used to offer in the days before Austerity. Blue-collar jobs were also boosted by the North Sea oil boom, especially around the construction yard at Arnish Point just across the bay from Stornoway.

Stornoway therefore has changed. The council itself is the only authority with a Gaelic name: Comhairle nan Eilean Siar (it translates, unsurprisingly, as the Western Isles Council). The town marches on, though the current round of service cuts brought on by Austerity is having an impact. But the spirt of Stornoway is unquenchable.

The town has a complicated relationship with landward Lewis. Stornoway at one time was perversely proud of not being a majority Gaelic-speaking community, unlike the 'maws' who flocked in from the country for secondary school education, or just a job. (The etymology is debateable, but I was taught in the days of my youth that it was a corruption of the name Maoris, the indigenous people of New Zealand. I blush for shame.)

The country folk had little love for these stuck-up Stornowegians. I remember, as a child, running into a Sunday school picnic from somewhere in the hinterland at a local beach, and being given ice cream by a young lady, who was dishing it out to the other youngsters. Where did I come from, she asked. Stornoway, I told her. 'If I'd known that', she scowled, 'you'd have got no ice cream from me.' These days things are better integrated. Though maybe not the Niseachs.

During World War I many inhabitants of the island enlisted as combatants. It was, therefore, a tragic irony that, on 31 December 1918 ('Hogmanay'), a ship carrying Lewis men back from the conflict collided with rocks near the entrance to Stornoway Harbour and quickly sunk in the deep waters. The HMS Iolaire was piloted by a Royal Navy crew, who were unfamiliar with the passage from Ullapool, and there were only enough lifeboats and jackets available for the crew.

If the Navy crew had turned the pilotage over to the ship's passengers, this accident would almost certainly not have occurred. However, they didn't, and over 250 local men drowned in front of their families standing on the pier waiting to welcome them home. This tragedy continues today to resonate deeply within the local community.

A few years earlier, Stornoway and Lewis had been affected by The Clearances, though to a lesser extent than the mainland. The Liberal government passed the Crofters Act in 1886. However, shortly afterwards, a Conservative government was elected and, being naturally allied with the landowning classes, they did their best to nullify the positive effects of the Act on the people. In the winter of 1887/88 the government sent a military force to Lewis to quell the crofters' anger. At Aignish Farm near Stornoway, there was hand-to-hand fighting between the local Land League members and the infantry.

In the early years of the 20th century, a fall in agricultural commodity prices in the wake of World War I seriously affected the Highland economy, and several hundred people left Stornoway by boat for what they hoped would be a more prosperous future in America.

Recently, however, the impact of the oil industry and the fostering of agricultural reforms have led to the development of a more stable economy on the Western Isles and in Stornoway. The town's harbour today shows little sign of economic decline, with the constant comings and goings of fishing fleets, a marina for private boats, a shipyard and slipway, a lifeboat station and three piers for commercial traffic.

The Cal Mac ferry, the 320-feet 'Isle of Lewis', had long operated out of the harbour on its regular trips to Ullapool. In January 2015 its replacement, the £42 million 380-feet 'Loch Seaforth', sparked local outrage when it was discovered that this new ferry didn't have a bar on board. A councillor said: 'it's scandalous spending millions on a ferry with no bar', to which Cal Mac replied that this reflects a 'change in public taste'. Did they ask any of the public if their taste had changed? It certainly hadn't changed in Stornoway.

Busted Bothans

The ancient Gaelic toast is 'slainte mhath' – you may find it useful – which of course translates as 'good health'. But back in the middle of the 20th century, there was little that was particularly healthy in many of the drinking establishments outside Stornoway.

In those days, most of the island was composed of dry parishes, so you couldn't combine drink and socialising unless you went to Stornoway. Therefore, there sprung up – or perhaps staggered up – a series of entirely illegal drinking clubs in many of these parishes. They might have been situated in a corrugated iron shieling (summer places for sheep herders), outhouses, garages or sometimes someone's home. The bothan owners would take copious carry-outs from Stornoway and sell drink to their customers, without a licence.

In the 1970s, the police decided to bear down on the bothans. They busted one at Europie in Port of Ness, where, according to reports at the time, they found ten 11-gallon kegs of beer, 415 unopened cans of beer, as well as around 90 that were open, and various quantities of whisky and rum. Twenty-six locals were in the bothan, trying to drink it all. There were also some coins in a box.

The police officer in charge of the raid was asked what he'd made of that. In Sherlockian tones that were to ring round the islands to gales of laughter, he responded: 'I came to the conclusion that this was a place used for drinking'. The accused were found guilty and fined. And, in these more liberal licensing times, Ness now has a fine fully licensed social club.

Culturally, Stornoway has much to offer.

A distinctive arts centre, 'An Lanntair', opened in the Town Hall in 1985, so 2015 was its 30th anniversary. In 2005 it moved to its current location on the sea front, and it offers art, drama, film and a cafe. Lewis Loom Centre on Bayhead provides a history of Harris Tweed manufacture, with guided tours and lectures.

Museum nan Eilan contains an admirable collection of artefacts relating to Lewis and Hebridean history. The Museum was refurbished in early 2015 and is an extension to the restored Lews Castle ('Caistel Leodhais'), a category A listed building completed in 1857.

Flower Showers

One of the finest sights in all the Western Isles is to be found in places like Harris (also in parts of Lewis, and Uist to the south). The machair is, classically, a low-lying grassy plain, mostly to be found on the west coast of the aforementioned Islands, just above the sea. Sand, mostly crushed sea shells, is blown ashore by the Atlantic seas and, with the help of crofting practices, these grasslands have developed on and among the dunes.

Here you will see Hebridean wildflowers in profusion, and there are birds and insect life through the summer months, which again are very much natives of the machair. It's the sheer abundance of the flowers that make the grasslands a remarkable sight, and the machair typically changes colour through the season: yellow for a few weeks, then red, then white and blue.

It's an amazing visual experience, and there are various places to see it. But the best in Lewis and Harris is at Northton ('Taobh Tuath' – remember many road signs in the islands are in Gaelic), where corncrakes and breeding waders arrive in the spring and geese, and golden plover and lapwings are winter visitors. There are bumble bees and the Belted Beauty Moth, if you're into other airborne life forms. And if you walk out the Toe Peninsula, there's a profusion of white beaches, a ruined mediaeval chapel ('Rubh' an Teampaill') and stunning views from the top of the mountain Ceapabhal.

Finally, please be advised that adherents to the strict Presbyterian tenets of the Free Church of Scotland (universally known as 'Wee Frees') remain an influential presence in Stornoway. The Sabbath is widely observed in the town, with most of the shops closed and Sunday newspapers difficult to obtain. Indeed, it was not until July 2009 that the first ferry left Stornoway for Ullapool on a Sunday.

So, with the exception of Sundays, which are not exactly buzzing with social activities, you will certainly enjoy relaxing in this friendly Western Isles port, and using it as a base for discovering the rest of the island, including visits to the remarkable Standing Stones of Callanish on the west coast of Lewis and to the nearby rocky inlets and beaches of this beautiful land.

TAIN:

THE OLDEST ROYAL BURGH

I always managed to avoid Tain on my frequent car journeys on the old A9 to Sutherland and Caithness. Not that there was anything wrong with Tain: it was just easier that way.

Before the Dornoch Firth Bridge was opened in 1991, a left turn just after Evanton led one over the windy moorland of the Struie to rejoin the northbound A9 just before Bonar Bridge. This cut out the longer, more circuitous trip via Tain. Although today one still bypasses Tain on the A9, it's not by very much. So rather late in life, I've discovered that Tain is an intriguing place.

This town of some 3,500 people sits on the southern shore of the Dornoch Firth. A winter walk along some of its more exposed streets, with the wind and rain lashing off the North Sea, can be a freezing experience. But at warmer times of the year, such a promenade is often bracingly enjoyable.

The name 'Tain' is probably from the Old Norse 'thing' ('council'), as the town was taken over by Norway's Earl Sigurd in the 9th century and used as a Norse command post. In Gaelic, Tain is called 'Baile Dubhthaich' or 'Duthac's Town', Duthac being a priest who was born here, and who was created a saint in 1419. A Chapel was erected in the town in his honour.

Tain is the oldest Royal Burgh in Scotland, its Charter granted by King Malcolm III in 1066. This confirmed Tain as a 'sanctuary' where people could claim church protection or 'immunity' and where residents and traders could claim exemption from certain taxes. The centre of the sanctuary was the early Duthac Chapel.

Robert the Bruce sent his wife and daughter here for their safety in 1306, although they were snatched by the Earl of Ross and imprisoned in England for a number of years. The Chapel was burnt down during a clan feud in 1427 but was rebuilt, and it became Scotland's most important pilgrimage site, with King James IV an annual devotee.

The centre of Tain was dominated by a large Tollbooth, built in 1630. In 1650 James Graham, the pro-Royalist Marquis of Montrose, spent a night here on his way to his execution in Edinburgh after losing the Battle of Carbisdale to the Covenanters. The Tollbooth was damaged by Cromwell's troops who were quartered here in 1656 and incapable of behaving themselves, and it was then destroyed by fire in 1696.

A replacement was completed in 1733, and it was employed mainly as an administrative centre to try and, almost without exception, convict 'seditious' crofters who, as with many of their fellows in the Highlands, were savagely treated in Easter Ross during The Clearances.

Old Boys

Among the distinguished former citizens of Tain was Peter Fraser, who became Prime Minister of New Zealand between 1940 and 1949. Today, there's a statue of him in the Government Buildings Reserve in Wellington.

John Ross, a merchant, emigrated to the American colonies in the 18th century, and became embroiled in the American War of Independence, where he was appointed by Congress to the job of buying clothes, weapons and powder from France for the rebels. He was a friend of George Washington and Benjamin Franklin.

James Munro was a Presbyterian minister who fought against King James VI of Scotland (later also James I of England) over the monarch's attempts to unite Scotland's Presbyterian Church with England's Episcopal Church, in 1605. He died in Tain around 1630.

The Far North Line was opened in Tain by Highland Railway in 1864 and was acquired by LMS Railways in 1923. In World War II an aerodrome large enough for bombers was built at nearby 'Fendom', and the flat beaches around Inver, five miles to the west, were ideal for D-Day Landing exercises, much to the inconvenience of the local residents who had to find accommodation elsewhere. After the War the aerodrome was acquired by the Royal Navy Fleet Air Arm and then by the RAF.

Say Cheese

One of Tain's not-so-hidden jewels is a cheese company. Highland Fine Cheeses is a family business, established in 1963, which manufactures traditional cheeses unique to the Highlands and Islands of Scotland. The family owned the local dairy, so the raw material was available.

The company was set up by Reggie Stone, a Tain councillor whose ancestors were Provosts of the town, and his wife Susannah. Susannah Stone, a formidable woman, used to make crowdie – a soft and crumbly Highland cheese – at home in the 1960s, souring fresh milk by warming it on the window sill or in front of a fire, then cooking it till it curdled.

Mrs Stone separated the curds and whey over the bath and, when she'd made too much, she'd flog it off to the local grocer. So Highland Fine Cheeses was born, and prospered. Among their specialities is Caboc, a soft cheese rolled in pinhead oatmeal, which the company claims to have re-invented from an ancient recipe; Black Crowdie, covered in oatmeal and black pepper; and a variety of blue cheeses.

Mrs Stone took over the running of the company when Reggie died suddenly, and drove it to success. She was also a fervent campaigner against breast cancer, and got into enormously entertaining local battles with the medical profession when she launched a public campaign to buy breast-screening machines to instal in local hospitals, because the health authority hadn't. She was not a woman who took 'no' for an answer.

When she died in 2015, her son Rory (Ruaridh), who had formerly been a disc jockey and presenter with the local Moray Firth Radio, took over as artisan cheese maker. He came close to falling out with his brother Jamie, who was fighting the local Scottish parliamentary constituency for the Liberal Democrats, when Rory announced his support for the SNP candidate, rather than for his brother.

Jamie lost. He subsequently became a member of Highland Council, but was selected as Lib Dem Scottish Parliamentary candidate once again in 2016. The Stones are probably far too civilised to fall out forever over politics, but they are nothing if not entertaining. And their cheese is good.

In breaking news, Ruaridh is now (summer 2016) working on producing Scotland's smelliest cheese. It's to be called the Minger. A Minger is, according to which dictionary you consult, an ugly or smelly person. It sounds promising....

Agriculture, tourism, pottery and crafts are some of Tain's industries, and so is the mussel trade. The largest Common Mussel beds in Scotland lie in the Dornoch Firth near Tain. In 1612, King James VI granted to the Royal Burgh of Tain the ownership of all mussel 'scalps' ('beds') in the Firth and the right to fish for them. Mussels have always been an important source of food for the people of Tain, although today 60% of the catch is exported to France.

Much of the Dornoch Firth is a Marine Special Area of Conservation, and the mussels are left to grow in the wild where they naturally regenerate. The trade supports a number of jobs in the town, with the income going to the Tain Common Good Fund.

Another (very) important employer is the whisky industry. The world-renowned Glenmorangie Distilery is based here in what the locals call the 'Glen of Tranquility'. Glenmorangie's classic 10-year-old Highland Single Malt is revered by whisky lovers. The Balblair Distillery, five miles to the east of the town in Edderton ('the parish of peats') and equally favoured by connoisseurs of a 'wee dram', was established in 1790. It moved to its present site in 1895.

The Tain Highland Gathering every August is sponsored by Glenmorangie and is held in the grounds of the distillery, while the annual summer Tain Gala includes events ranging from fiddle playing competitions via eightsome reels to Red Arrow displays. 'Tain Through Time', located in St Duthus Collegiate Church, does exactly what it says on the tin, and the Museum, opened in 1966 contains archives, artefacts and exhibitions relating to the town.

Old Tom Morris won the Open Golf Championship at Prestwick four times in the 1860s and, in between his victories, he found the time to design Tain's golf course. This links course, as I have discovered to my cost, is almost as difficult to play as Royal Dornoch across the Firth. The word 'challenging' does not do this course full justice, and it is a test of nerve and skill in this most noble of all sports.

Some ten miles to the east of Tain is the fishing village of Portmahomack, which is not, as it may sound, the name of an Amerindian chief, but derives from the Gaelic 'Port Mo Chalmaig' ('home of St Colmac'). In the 19th century, the village was the centre for the white fish industry. It was claimed that the bay was then so full of boats that you could walk across the harbour without getting your feet wet. The village was also the site of the first Pictish monastery, built around 550 AD and destroyed by fire almost 300 years later.

The Tarbat Discovery Centre contains, among other fascinating items, fragments of Pictish stone sculptures. Portmahomack is today something of a tourist centre, offering a sandy beach, opportunities for watching dolphins, fishing and watersports. The 16th-century Ballone Castle, now restored, is nearby, while at the tip of the peninsula sits Tarbat Ness lighthouse.

Slightly further to the south is Hill of Fearn where Fearn Abbey was established in the 1220s. In 1742 the roof of the Abbey collapsed, killing numerous members of the congregation, but it was rebuilt by the Church of Scotland in 1772. On the coast close to Hill of Fearn is the fishing village of Balintore which was another important Pictish site, as were what are known as the surrounding 'Seaboard' villages. The Balintore seafront contains a plaque commemorating a local missionary named John Ross who was responsible in the 19th century for translating the Bible into Korean. Well, someone had to do it.

Seaboard saunter

If you travel from Tain to the south-east you'll come across what is called a 'hammerhead peninsula'. This contains what are known as the 'seaboard' villages: Hilton of Cadboll, Shandwick and Balintore.

These three settlements are separate in name but basically run into one another. All three were fishing villages, but none of them had a harbour. Local tradition speaks of boats being hauled up onto the shore, as far back, perhaps, as the era of the Vikings and their longships. Shandwick's name is thought to have been originally 'Sand Vik', the Old Norse for 'sand bay'.

On the hillside above Shandwick there's the Shandwick Stone ('Clach a'Charridh'), a stone cross which is housed these days in a large glass box. Since around 780 AD it served as a landmark for the fisher crews until it was broken in half in 1846,. Another Pictish cross was found near Hilton of Cadboll beside the buried remains of a chapel. Nearby, bumps in a field are thought to be the remains of the mediaeval village of Cadboll-Fisher.

Today, Balintore has a harbour, built in the 1890s, but there's a sense here that these are villages just slightly out of time. They also have a mermaid. The Mermaid of the North is eight feet high and weighs in at 800 pounds. It was originally made by Steven Hayword from Hilton but was badly damaged in the storms of 2012. It's since been recast in bronze.

THURSO:
ON TOP OF THE WORLD

How many British placenames can you name ending with the letter 'O'? There's Truro, Kelso, Portobello... and then it becomes tricky, until you consider the North-East Highlands of Scotland, where you have Embo, Skibo, Skelbo, Culbo and plenty others.

Why? Because Caithness and parts of Sutherland were under Norse occupation for centuries, and the Norse word 'bol' or 'bo' means 'large fertile farm' (the 'L' gradually disappeared except, oddly enough, in Eriboll, in the northwest of Sutherland: a Gaelic stronghold). And then there's Thurso.

Caithness (from 'Cait' for when it was a Pictish province and 'ness' from Old Scots for a promontory) is a linguistic anomaly in the Highlands of Scotland, given the county's minimal recourse to the Gaelic tongue. Indeed, until the mid-13th century most inhabitants of this austere, windswept but surprisingly fertile (in places) land were Norse, or 'Norn', speakers who identified more with the Norse Earldom of Orkney than they did with Scotland.

Ee Language

Reluctant as I am to dispute my esteemed colleague's recollections of his holiday stamping ground, the contention often aired in Caithness that Gaelic was never spoken there is contradicted by the many Gaelic place names still splattered across the county. In fact, Gaelic and Norse co-existed for centuries in Caithness, whichever came first.

But there is a Caithness language. Boring people might insist it's only a dialect, but the Caithness tongue is something that stands on its own, and can leave the careless eavesdropper with a slightly scrambled brain. It undoubtedly takes some of its word forms from the Shetland and Orkney Islands to the north, where the lingo undoubtedly has Norse roots, and has similarities to the north-east Doric, but it's very much its own beast.

The Scots Language Centre's guide to all of this though gives you a few clues. In Caithness, the 'wh' sound (what, when) is pronounced as an 'f' (fan, fat). Caithness speakers sometimes say 'she', 'her' or hers' rather then 'it' and 'its'. And then there's 'the'. In Caithness, you say 'ee' rather than 'the' (though it's sometimes shown as 'e'). Hence the title of this article.

If you want to appreciate the full magnificence of ee language, then here is an extract from the beginning of E Silkie Man *by David Houston, which you can find on the aforementioned Scots Language website:*

"So Donel' an' Peter 'ey pits on 'eir keps an' ey're aff owre 'e links is hard is 'ey can pin, t' see fat's come o'r. 'Ey pairted at 'e point 'e Niss, Donel' he meed aist aboot fill he cam' t' Sannick, an' Peter he geed wast aboot fill he meed Robby's hevn. 'Ey searched ivry hol an' corner. 'Ey cried an''ey fustled, bit 'ere's nee try nor token o' Kirsty. An noo' is 'ey cam back t' far 'ey pairted, 'ere 'e fowg lifts, an' 'e shore's a' ifore 'em bit id's 'e same teel...

Would you like a nice lie down now ?

By the 15th century Broad Scots was challenging the Norn dialect. In 1469 King James III's marriage to the daughter of the King of Norway brought Orkney and Shetland permanently under the control of Scotland. Gaelic was by now virtually absent except in the far west of the county, and Scots became the accepted language of Caithness by the 17th century.

The two largest settlements in Caithness have always been the ports of Wick on the east and Thurso on the north coasts. Thurso was originally known as Tarvadubron (early Celtic for 'bull water') and, after the Viking invasions of the 9th century, it became the Norse Thjorsa, later adapted to Thorsa ('Thor's river'). Its Gaelic name of 'Inbhir Theorsa' is of comparatively recent origin.

Today, Thurso stands at the junction of the A836 (a continuation of the A9) from Duncansby Head and the A882 from Wick, although it can also be reached across the treeless interior via the A895 from Latheron: a road which passes yards from my late Auntie Mary's house at Achavanich (Gaelic for 'field of stones') and which, from my childhood observations, witnessed the passage of roughly one vehicle per hour.

The most northerly town on the British mainland, with a population of around 10,000, Thurso possesses an extensive sandy beach and a natural deepwater harbour. It faces north over the unpredictable, stormy waters of the Pentland Firth (Pentland Fjord, as was) towards Orkney's Old Man of Hoy, a red sandstone, sheer rock stack, which was first climbed in 1966.

A roll-on, roll-off ferry from the town's harbour of Scrabster connects Thurso with Stromness in Orkney. It can be a harrowing voyage. A friend of mine was once on the ferry and commented to a ferry hand on the rough stormy weather. 'Just wait till we leave the harbour', he was told.

Thurso was inhabited at least 5000 years ago, as revealed by the Neolithic burial cairns at nearby Shebster Hill. For the Norse invaders it was an important port, the major gateway to mainland Scotland, and it continued to trade regularly with northern Europe until the 19th century. Such was the town's pivotal economic importance that, after Caithness became part of Scotland, King David II in 1330 brought Scotland's standard weight measures in line with those of Thurso.

By 1200 the increasingly powerful Scots monarchy was gradually imposing its bishops in the north of the country, supplanting the Norse Orcadian bishops, but encountering fierce resistance from the Earls of Orkney. In 1202 the Earls stormed the residence of the Scots bishop of Thurso, gouging out his eyes and ripping his tongue from his mouth.

Twenty years later his successor, Bishop Adam, was attacked and roasted to death in his own kitchen. The outraged King Alexander II headed north with an avenging army and dealt savagely with the perpetrators of the latter deed, ordering that 400 of them should be gelded as a punishment.

So it was with some relief that the Scottish bishopric greeted The Treaty of Perth, signed in 1266 between Norway and King William I, which recognised Caithness as part of Scotland and terminated this schism. Old St Peter's Kirk was founded in 1125 before this bloody period and remains in the centre of Thurso. Today, it is category A listed, boasts some handsome stained glass windows partly funded by philanthropist Andrew Carnegie, and is one of Scotland's oldest churches.

Two of the most common surnames in Thurso and, indeed, Caithness generally, are Gunn and Sinclair, although MacKay is close behind. Clan Gunn, one of the oldest Scottish clans, is descended from the Norse Jarls and the Pictish Mormaers (governors) of Caithness. The Sinclairs are of French origin and became Earls of Orkney before assuming the Earldom of Caithness in 1455, a position they continue to hold today. One of the most significant challenges they have faced was in the mid-17th century when the Irish attacked Thurso, but the aggressors were beaten back by Sir James Sinclair. Internecine feuds continued for many years between the Orcadian and Caithness branches of the Sinclairs.

Today, Thurso is a relatively prosperous town, with most of it planned and designed in the 19th century. Its economy has traditionally been based on sheep farming, forestry, linen cloth, tanning and fishing out of Scrabster harbour, while in the 19th century the flagstone and slate industry employed over 1000 people. Caithness slate remains popular today as a building material for walls, hearths and kitchen workshops, and the locals use it for building dykes.

The town enjoyed a boom period from the mid-1950s when the Dounreay nuclear facility, nine miles to the west of the town, was being constructed. Dounreay was originally an old castle: its name derives from the Gaelic for 'fort on a mound'. Between 1955 and 1958 the population of the town rose from 2,500 to 12,000 (the Dounreay workers were known locally as 'the atomic people'). In 1994, the government ordered the reactors to be decommissioned, a process which will not be complete until at least 2125.

In 2010 permission was granted for the development of a 21-turbine wind farm in the Thurso area. Also, plans are in place for putting the Thurso area in the forefront of wave energy technology which, given the strong currents of the Pentland Firth, should provide the required energy power.

The town is home to North Highland College, part of the University of the Highlands and Islands, and the refurbished Old Town Hall on the High Street contains the Caithness Horizons Museum, which displays an impressive 8,500 historical artefacts relating to the region. As with many similar Highland towns, Thurso has produced a diverse collection of alumni, including Boys Brigade founder Sir William Alexander Smith, General and friend of George Washington during the American War of Independence Arthur St Clair, celebrated 19th-century geologist and botanist Robert Dick whose herbarium is in the Museum, and ex-Scottish international and Norwich City goalie Brian Gunn.

The broad expanse of Thurso Bay is also ideal for surfing and kayaking and has hosted the European Surfing Championships. If none of this appeals to you, there is always the Thurso Pipe Band, a popular attraction in the town.

Making A Splash

Thurso is a surfing mecca. Yes, really. At first sight, you might think this is not obviously the land of bronzed beach bums and golden girls in bikinis. You'd be right.

But the surf at Thurso East is special, according to those who know. It's a 'fast reef break', which I just about understand, and it's Scotland's prime surfing venue on the north coast. It's 'primarily a long walling right-hander with several barrel sections, depending on tide and swell directions'. Nope, now I'm losing it.

What I can tell you is that it was the venue for the O'Neill Highland Open in 2006 and, in subsequent years, played host to something called the Coldwater Classic, which entirely lived up to its name, but still attracted golden boys and girls in pickups and beach buggies, and some of the world's top surfers. O'Neill have now moved on.

What I can tell you too is that it remains spectacular surfing country. What I would advise you is that, as well as the wet suit, some sort of thermal clothing under that suit would be advisable. It's chilly out there.

The Far North Coast

There is a recent marketing campaign you may have come across concerning the Far North of mainland Scotland. North Coast 500 (with whom, incidentally, we have absolutely no connection) suggests you travel round the west coast, the north coast and finally the east coast from Inverness, sampling the scenery, the people and the various commercial premises out here at the mysterious edge of the world. It is, say the marketeers, the 'Route 66 of Scotland':

We propose you sample at least a taste of this scenario. However, to avoid confusion with this admirable initiative, unlike North Coast 500 which recommends making the round trip from west to east, we suggest a trip westwards out of Thurso across 'the top of the world', or at least along the Far North coast of Scotland.

This is another of Scotland's largely unknown wildernesses: scoured by the wind, beaten by the surf, and prone to spectacularly speedy changes in weather, as the wind blows in yet another front from America. It is remote, this craggy coastline, but it is not as empty as you might expect.

*In **Bettyhill,** there's the Strathnaver Museum which documents The Clearances in that sad strath, as well as its more mystical past; there's the village of **Tongue** (which has given rise to some regrettable car stickers: figure it out) with the mighty mountains of Ben Loyal and Ben Hope towering over its sweeping causeway; **Melvich,** with its golden beach; and **Portskerra**, with its Drowning Monument. And there's **Globland**.*

*You will not find that name on the map. But on the A838, beyond Tongue, you will come to **Loch Eriboll**. Lotte Glob is a Danish ceramic artist and sculptor who lives in a house at the southern end of the Loch. If you keep an eye out, you will not miss it, given the spectacular ceramics on the gate posts. Inside, you'll drive into a strange and spooky wonderland, populated by odd beasties and petrified water fountains that she has designed: Lotte Glob's Sculpture Croft.*

Here, there's plenty to see and lots to buy, if you like what's on show. But, here's a warning: I have visited this croft on a number of occasions, but I have never actually met her. There is a big golden bell outside her showroom and you could try ringing that. She may come. But the chances are she'll be somewhere out on the hills with her latest sculpture, looking for the right place to install it. These journeys can take several days. Strange figurines adorn moonscape mountain sides, while floating 'stones' bob on lonely lochans. If you're of a hill walking disposition, you may come across them. They're Lotte's.

*As you head west from Loch Erribol, you will see a sign alerting you to **Smoo Cave**. Wander down a wooden staircase in the cliff, and you come out at sea level. However, beware the tide. When it's in, there are boat trips into the cavern. When it's out, you can walk in through the largest cave entrance in Britain. It's over 120 feet wide and 15 feet high.*

The first main chamber has been formed by the sea. But beyond it there is a second chamber, and that has been gouged out of the limestone by rainwater. Right at the back of this chamber, which you approach by a covered wooden walkway, a 60-feet-high waterfall, created by the overflowing waters of the Alt Smoo burn, thunders down, wafting what looks like steam throughout the cave. It's very dramatic, and feels very underground.

Historically, Smoo was supposed to be the entrance to the underworld. The cave, which may also have been used for smuggling, definitely saw another sort of spirit, as it was used by locals for illegal distilling. Indeed, a local man is said to have drowned two nosey excise officers here. Also, a famed highwayman called MacMurdo supposedly threw his victims down the blowhole at the top of the cave. (We'll meet this charming gentleman again.) Finally, invading members of Clan Gunn were murdered to the last man in Smoo Cave. So watch yourself.

*It's definitely a recommended stop on your north coast trip, as is the nearby **Sango Beach**, which you can access from a car park at the Tourist Information Centre. It has cliffs and sand dunes and rock formations growing out of the beach like the fossils of strange Jurassic beasts. Which they sort of are, of course.*

*Beyond Smoo and Sango, you'll come to the crofting village of **Durness.** You can see why locals sometimes describe it as 'the last outpost'. It's actually a string of crofting townships laced together along the coast. Sheep farming still goes on around here and, if you're unlucky, you might get stuck on one of the single-track roads behind a flock of homeward-bound sheep. The last time this happened to me, they were being herded by a man on a beach buggy.*

*Travel through the village to the former military base which is now **Balnakiel Craft Village**. In this faintly hippy settlement of arts and crafts people are some of the best chocolates you'll ever buy, as well as wonderful hot chocolate drinks. Look for Cocoa Mountain. You'll thank me afterwards.*

*Beyond the Craft Village, you'll come to a ruined church, a graveyard, and a rolling white beach, heading out through the dunes to the peninsula of **Faraid Head**. Also here is the hulking Balnakiel House, built on the ruins of the summer palace of the Bishop of Caithness..*

Buried among the tombs in the churchyard across the way are the great Gaelic poet Rob Donn and the highwayman MacMurdo (or MacMurchow) whom we last met at Smoo Cave. He is said to have murdered 18 people, and he was buried here after he paid the church for a plot. There's also, in a mass grave, a crew whose ship sank off Faraid Head in 1843.

*Some days here, you will hear in the distance the crump and bang of military armaments, because beyond Balnakiel, there's **Cape Wrath**, where the military still play wargames on the local range. It takes a bus, a boat and another bus to get to Cape Wrath, but you can hire a place aboard.*

In 2010, Kay Ure, who lived with her husband John at the old lighthouse keeper's cottage, popped out to get a Christmas turkey in Inverness: a trip involving an 11-mile drive to the ferry, then a minibus onwards from the other side. It was 23 December. Having got the festive bird, Mrs Ure then set off for home, but got no further than Durness. Heavy snow had made the rest of the journey impossible, and so Mr Ure spent Christmas at home with the dogs, and no festive grub. By the time the snow cleared, it was late January. The Ures finally got to celebrate Christmas 30 days after everyone else. It would be as well to bear this in mind if you're planning a trip that way in winter. There's a limit to just how much White Christmas anyone would want. Ask John Ure.

*Beyond, you'll come to one of Europe's busiest fishing ports, at **Kinlochbervie**. The most northerly port on Scotland's West Coast, the village's website boasts that it is the last place you come to before falling into the sea. Set amid the crags and peaks of the North-West Geopark, it was listed by the Oxford English Dictionary as a definition of the word 'remote'. The cinema arrives on the back of a lorry, and so does the bank. But it's a busy, vital community and worth a visit, to watch the boats going in and out, in just about all weathers. Here they really know the price of fish.*

And now you're moving south into the lands of Assynt, which is where this book begins. Welcome back.

TORRIDON:
MAJESTIC WESTERN WILDERNESS

The spectacularly mountainous landscape around the village of Torridon in Wester Ross can justifiably claim, along with Assynt further to the north, to possess the most unspoilt and breathtaking landscape in the British Isles.

Located at the foot of Upper Loch Torridon, Torridon village, known until the 1950s as 'Fasag' and whose name today derives from the Old Norse for 'the loch of Thorfinn's town' or, in Gaelic, 'Toirbheartan', lies only 80 miles west from the busy city of Inverness but such is the contrast in their environments that they could almost be a planet's distance apart. This comparison is not intended to denigrate the Inverness area (would I dare?) which is also set against a stunning, natural backdrop, but rather to emphasise the extraordinary beauty of Torridon.

The long sea inlet Loch Torridon also contains the smaller Loch Shieldaig (Old Norse for 'loch of the herring'), and is presided over by some of Britain's highest mountains, made up of Torridian Sandstone and which are, at between 300 and 500 million years old, among the oldest rocks in Europe. Four of the mountains are 'Munros' (over 3,000 feet high): Liathach ('the grey one'), Beinn Alligin ('jewelled mountain'), Sgorr Ruadh ('the red peak') and Maol Chean Dearg ('bald red head') soar up, in some cases almost vertically, from the lochs and glens of the Torridon wilderness.

The climate is a bit warmer here than in the Eastern Highlands, as the coast of Torridon is on the Atlantic Gulf Drift, but the rainfall is significantly higher than in more inland areas. However, as an experienced hill walker of my acquaintance once said: 'there is no such thing as bad weather, just bad clothing'. Eh?

Torridon's isolation encourages the presence of an impressive diversity of wildlife, as humans are rather thin on the ground, although there are several walks for those fortunate enough to visit the area. On the northern shore of the

Loch, just west of Torridon, sits Inver Alligin, with a natural cave ('Smuggler's Cave') once used by locals trying to avoid the attentions of the sharp-eyed excisemen, and which offers, on clear days, grand views of Skye to the west. The main road stops at Diabeg ('deep bay'), another lovely wee village but which had the misfortune to be used as the setting for the execrable movie 'Loch Ness'.

The road westward on the southern shore passes through the village of Shieldaig, now a fishing port mainly for prawns and mussels. Shieldaig was originally designed and laid out by the British government to train soldiers for the Napoleonic Wars (Highlanders have a well-earned reputation as, to use an Old Scots phrase, 'bonny fechters': 'good fighters'). However, as the village's construction did not begin until 1810, the men of Shieldaig were too late to enter that particular fray.

Crew Cut Island

Shieldaig is one of these beautiful hidden gems you're liable to come across only by accident or if you're familiar with the byways as well as the highways of the West Coast. There are fantastic views to enjoy as you wend your way down to the village on the banks of Loch Shieldaig, itself a tributary of the sea loch, Loch Torridon.

As well as the striking vistas of the mountains across the water, and as well as truly spectacular sunsets, you may notice an island that looks rather like a crew cut haircut, attached to a Dennnis the Menace character lurking just below the waves. In fact, it's Shieldaig Island, which is densely packed with mature Scots pine, thought to have been planted with seed from Strathspey in the 19th century, and it contrasts fairly dramatically with the bare hillsides round about. The plan is gradually to replace them with native Highland pines, though that may take a couple of hundred years or so.

Time moves differently in the West Highlands.

A new road was laid down in 1975 around the Applecross Peninsula from Shieldaig to Loch Kishorn where an oilrig fabrication yard operated between 1975 and 1987. The Howard Doris yard at Kishorn was responsible for creating *the largest man-made structure ever to move across the surface of planet Earth. (I do not exaggerate here, which is why it's in italics.)* The Ninian Central Concrete Platform required seven large tugs to move it from Loch Kishorn to its operating station in the North Sea.

The new road from Shieldaig is single-track, and it snakes, often tortuously, around the outer edge of the peninsula, so think twice about taking a caravan. It also provides some of the finest views in Britain. It travels south through the towering Bealach na Ba ('pass of the cattle'), is the highest road in Britain and is probably the closest you will get in this country to an Alpine pass. It stops at the little coastal village of Applecross.

Applecross Energy

There are many things to like about the village of Applecross: though some would dispute there is such a thing. Technically, Applecross is the name of the parish beyond the spectacular and breath-taking Bealach na Ba, mentioned by Rab, and the string of buildings curving round Applecross Bay is known to some locally as 'The Street', rather than as an actual village.

But get over that, and you will be able to feast not only on the sumptuous views out to the island of Raasay, but also on the spectacular seafood at the Applecross Inn. A short walk around the bay will take you to the Walled Garden, profusely perfumed and wonderfully sunny on a summer's day (well, some of them), part of the Applecross Estate, and home to the Potting Shed café.

And then there's the people. They're nothing if not enterprising here on the edge of the West Coast. For many years, the village had its own petrol pumps. Then, in 2008, the operator gave up the lease, and the locals (not to mention thousands of tourists) faced a 36-mile round trip to Lochcarron to fill up. So they decided to set up their own community company and raise funds in order to save the pumps.

They pulled together £16,000 from their own initial efforts and, with support from the Lottery Fund and the Scottish government among others, the petrol station was reopened in 2010 by the former leader of the Liberal Democrats, the late Charles Kennedy, who was then the area's MP. Today it's available 24/7 by means of a credit card machine.

Some of those involved in the pump-preservation campaign went on to another high energy project, christened Apple Juice. It's a hydroelectric company, aimed at constructing a 90-kilowatt scheme from the waters of the Allt Breugach burn which flows from the hills behind the village into Applecross Bay. And just five weeks after they announced a share issue in October 2015, the company had raised its target total of £78,000, many of the investors coming from the area.

169

Trust bust-up

There have also been the odd sparks flying in Applecross over the owners of the 61,000-acre estate. Officially, it's owned by the Applecross Trust. The Trust, at the time of writing, is chaired by a man called Richard Wills from Andover in Hampshire, who's a member of the Wills tobacco family. They bought the estate from the executors of the tenth Baron Middleton in 1924, and set up a Trust to run it in the 1980s. None of the seven present trustees lives in Applecross.

In 2012, a campaign group, Land Action Scotland, headed by the land researcher and campaigner Andy Wightman, who has written several books on land ownership matters in Scotland and runs his own highly regarded website on the subject, orchestrated a campaign for local people and others to apply for trusteeships.

The Trust hit back by producing a letter and petition, which claimed the majority of the people in the area wanted things left well alone. They refused to entertain the applications for trusteeships, despite the fact that they included their MP and MSP.

The campaigners finally withdrew from the row to avoid exacerbating community relations, but there is no doubt the community remains split over the issue. So, go carefully on this subject…

The A896 eastward from Torridon to Kinlochewe winds its way through the Beinn Eighe Natural Nature Reserve, designated in 1951 as the first such Reserve in Britain. A mile or two further along the road you'll find the Torridon Countryside Centre at Achnasheen, a handy source of information for visitors.

The Wrong Loch

The village of Kinlochewe is situated on the beautiful Loch Maree, possibly the most scenic stretch of water in the entire Highlands, and you should try to stop off in one of the many laybys to have a proper look at it.

But if you're a keen Gaelic scholar or even, like me, a lazy one, you may have spotted a puzzle. The word 'kin' in English placenames almost always denotes, through the Gaelic word 'ceann', a settlement that is at the head of something. In this case, therefore, the village should be at the head of Loch Ewe. But it isn't. It's at the head of Loch Maree.

The reason for that is that Loch Maree used to be known as Loch Ewe and was only renamed around 1700, to commemorate the Irish missionary St Mealrubha, who's said to have brought Christianity to the area, and had a cell on one of the islands in the Loch.

Towering over Loch Maree to the north-east you can't miss the spectacular mountain Slioch, a massive block of rock glowering at Kinlochewe and the Beinn Eighe Nature Reserve beyond. Rolling back from there, it's mountainous wilderness but, though there used to be a drove road over that side of the Loch, it's rugged country, so take care.

If you're a tree, Loch Maree is not good country for you. Early in the 1600s, English ironmasters set up on the shore and, for half a century, iron ore was imported into the area by sea, smelted on site and then shipped out again. This low-cost process came to an end when just about every tree in the area was burned. Eventually, trees were replanted, and all went well until World War II. Then somebody had a bright idea: and all the trees were chopped down again to make ammunition boxes.

Today, restocking seems to be under way again but, if I was a forest, I wouldn't be overconfident about the future.

The Clearances began in the Torridon area in 1831 when the estate was sold to one Colonel McBarnet, who had made his fortune in the West Indies slave plantations. His attitude to his Highland tenants was no doubt similar to his treatment of his slaves, as they were immediately stripped of their lands and they were 'relocated' to scrape a living at the relatively infertile head of the Loch. However, the Baron of Gourock then acquired the estate. He was a man of more liberal and humane sentiments. He returned the lands to his tenants and developed a deer forest.

Unlike the many unscrupulous landlords in the Highlands who were only interested in profiting from their properties and who ignored the needs and well-being of their tenants, Gourock also lent them money to buy cattle and boats. On his death in 1910 the National Trust took over the estate.

Beinn Eighe bomber

Beinn Eighe is historic in its own right, in that it was the first National Nature Reserve in the country, established in 1951. But there's also a tragic history attached to it.

In that same year, a converted Lancaster bomber was flying a maritime reconnaissance mission out to Rockall and the Faroe Islands. On its journey back to its north-east base at RAF Kinloss, it flew into freezing weather and strong headwinds in the darkness. Not long after it transmitted its last radio message, it flew into the Triple Buttress just 15 feet from the summit of Beinn Eighe (how close it came to missing the mountain altogether), crashing into the near-inaccessible Far West Gully, which in a grim postscript, came to be known as Fuselage Gully.

Search teams were dispatched, but couldn't find the aircraft in the area. Only a local boy, who'd spotted a red glow over the mountain, gave the authorities any sort of clue about where it was. Finally, another aircraft flew over the wreckage and reported its location. Even then, the rescue teams dispatched to the mountain couldn't get up there because of the atrocious weather and the challenging terrain. One search team member, remembering the incident many years later, said it was equivalent to going into the unknown in Scotland's largely uncharted mountains.

Ironically, their difficulties led to the setting up of RAF Mountain Rescue teams, which have since come to the aid of many civilians on Scotland's mountains. But back in 1951, it took two Royal Marine commandoes to retrieve the first bodies of the eight-strong crew from the mountain top, and nearly six months to get them all down, using horses to carry the bodies down the lower slopes. As a result of this incident, the Torridon Mountain Rescue Team was also set up.

In yet another irony, in 2008, a climber who fell on the mountain is said to have had his fall broken by one of the Lancaster's propellers. He was nonetheless seriously injured.

As for activities in the area, my own fondest memory is of staying for a short period in Torridon House, a splendid mansion overlooking Loch Torridon and which was owned by the Lovelace family. I played snooker much of the day on their handsome and impeccably-maintained table with a friend of mine who happened to be Lady Lovelace's chauffeur. (Sorry, Gordon, but I have to tell someone.) As such a facility is probably now beyond the scope of the visitor, I suggest that instead you make full use of the many available outdoor pursuits.

These include mountain climbing (but please ensure you are well trained and qualified in this rewarding but potentially hazardous pastime), hill walking (much easier), kayaking, sailing, fishing, whale watching, mountain biking and generally strolling around this most splendid of natural panoramas.

Every summer there is the Celtman Extreme Triathlon, which will test your fitness, while on the first two weeks of October there is the Torridon Mountain and Sea Festival whch incorporates all the above (aside from snooker) and also the Walking and Ale Festivals.

The Loch Torridon Community Centre, based in Torridon village, a community-owned venture, puts on various events, such as Scottish country dancing and weaving classes, and has a permanent photographic and art gallery. Many of the bars and hotels in the area have traditional and contemporary folk music evenings: indeed, a popular Highland folk/rock band is named Torridon as homage to the place. If you can't find a fascinating way of spending your time around Torridon, then you're not paying enough attention.

It is difficult to describe this remarkable area of the Highlands without resorting to even more platitudes and superlatives than I already have done, so I'll stop now. Suffice to say that, once you have travelled through this unique part of the Highlands, it is an experience you will not forget.

ULLAPOOL:
FISHING, FERRIES AND FESTIVALS

There are few other places in Scotland quite so friendly and welcoming as the port of Ullapool, which neatly encapsulates the Gaelic culture and vibrant spirit of the Western Highlands of Scotland.

For such a busy and interesting place, Ullapool is surprisingly remote, the nearest settlement of a comparable size being Gairloch which lies over 50 miles to the south by road. Ullapool's population of around 1,300 is usually considerably swollen in numbers by foreign fishermen and, in the summer, by hordes of tourists who descend on the place, which is a haven for wildlife enthusiasts, walkers, watersporters, birdwatchers and mountain climbers, and by those who just wish to experience the pristine air and peace of West Coast life. Ullapool is located on the warm North Atlantic Drift, so the weather and local flora are what one might expect to experience in more southerly climes.

The name of the town derives from the Gaelic 'Ulapul' which in turn has its origin in the Norse word for 'wool farm' or 'Ull's farm', as the Viking invaders of the 9th to 11th centuries inhabited much of the area north of a line drawn roughly from Ullapool to Dingwall.

Sitting on the eastern shore of Loch Broom (Little Loch Broom is a couple of miles south), the town as it is today was founded by the British Fisheries Society in 1788 as a herring port and was designed by Thomas Telford. A fishing settlement existed here for many centuries beforehand, dating back to the late Bronze Age and Iron Age, as the remains of stone buildings at Rhue, two miles north of Ullapool, have revealed to archaeologists.

After World War II, the size of the harbour was doubled to accommodate the growing number of fishing boats attracted by the variety and quantity of fish and shellfish in both Loch Broom and the waters of The Minch.

In the late 1960s and 1970s large Scandinavian factory ships, known as 'klondykers', began to moor in Loch Broom, and they were later joined by Eastern European factory ships in search of the teeming shoals of mackerel, as well as by vessels from Ireland, Nigeria, France and Japan.

Iain, who reported regularly for BBC Scotland on the 'klondyke' phenomenon, here explains what happened.

A City On The Sea

If you approach the port of Ullapool from the south-east it bursts on you as a surprise, even when you know it's there. Round a bend, and there's the planned grid of mostly white buildings clustered round Loch Broom, shining in even a winter sun, with boats tied up alongside the harbour, and maybe the equally white ferry, leaving for, or arriving from, the Hebridean port of Stornoway.

If you'd come round that same bend between the late 1970s and the early 1990s, you would have seen a very different sight. This was a city on the sea. You'd have seen a vast flotilla of large industrial ships – anything up to 70 at a time – with most of Scotland's fishing fleet pulling in alongside these huge, often rusting hulks, while little sea-taxi boats buzzed in and out and around them. These were the days of the Klondyke.

Unlike the Yukon gold rush from which this event took its name, this was based around fish. Mackerel are highly prized all over the earth's oceans, and their migration paths from west to east led a long trail of fishers in their wake. Behind them, the factory ships who bought the catches for top dollar, processed them and shipped them home to Europe, to Africa and Eastern Europe. During these years, that trail led to Ullapool.

At least half the sea-going nations of the world sent their boats to Loch Broom. The most conspicuous were those who came from Eastern Europe. In the 1980s in particular, the Cold War was at its height, but Ullapool was a 24/7 city on the sea, where sailors from the USSR, and many of its satellite nations, came together with West Highlanders, at all times of day and night.

They did so literally on one occasion when a team of Soviet sailors took on Ullapool at football, borrowing boots from the locals. Such was the world-wide controversy it caused – it was seen by the Daily Mails of this world as constituting a threat to Western civilisation – that it was the first and last such game played in Ullapool.

The presence of all these craft from behind the Iron Curtain filled the headlines. And sometimes they didn't. The only time I was ever served with a D-notice, which was a government order prohibiting you from reporting something on the grounds of national security, was when I found out that a crew member from an east European vessel had defected and asked for political asylum. I was ordered not to mention it, and the BBC would certainly not report it. So, to this day I have no idea whether the government was being paranoid, or whether my defector came with strategically important information.

A woman of my acquaintance remembers her first sight of the phenomenon, when driving into Ullapool and coming across a black man sitting on a wall, leafing through an Argos catalogue. This was not a sight you came across in West Highland villages, and it flags up the other big impact of the Klondyke on Ullapool: shopping.

Shops in Ullapool were stripped of produce. One proprietor claimed that he had to remove any clear glass bottles containing clear liquid, such as turpentine or ammonia, because Russian crews would assume it was vodka, and slip it onto their shopping. A local businessman told me how he'd been offered an unusual payment for his services aboard an Egyptian vessel, when a crewman slipped up behind him, as he spoke to the captain, and slipped a large chunk of cannabis into his open mouth.

Klondyke crews would descend, in hired mini-buses, on white goods shops as far away as Inverness, and bear away washing machines, fridges and televisions. One of my contacts swore blind he watched a Soviet ship heading for home: lashed down on the deck, was not only half a kitchen, but two brand-new Skoda cars: coals to Newcastle, perhaps, but very saleable on the streets of Odessa.

I made a BBC Radio Scotland programme about the klondyke boom, during which we went to the rescue of a drifting boat on a rough sea. That programme was eventually broadcast across the globe on the BBC's World Service, such was the fascination with the klondykers.

My young sons came back from visiting friends in Ullapool, with their pockets full of cash in half a dozen different currencies, slipped into their paws by sentimental seamen missing their own families.

The klondyke eventually ended. The mackerel altered their migration path and the boom moved to Lerwick in Shetland, before leaving Scottish shores altogether. Ullapool, though, still has the memories and still feels the benefits.

One sea-taxi operator became, for a time, an agent for the Soviet fleet, and once showed me a movement chart for the ships for which he was responsible, scattered around the globe, and insured for millions of pounds. Money made from the Klondyke helped build Ullapool's UK award-winning Seaforth Inn, Bistro and Chippy on the seafront. The Chippy is worth a visit, and so too is the Ceilidh Place, a magnet for musicians from all over the world to come and perform. It was named Venue of the Year in the 2014 Scottish Traditional Music Awards. It features a small number of rooms and a capacious bunk house.

Opened in a boat house by the actor Robert Urquhart, who was born in Ullapool, and his wife Jean, who subsequently became a Member of the Scottish Parliament, it has a charm all of its own, and its New Year celebrations are legendary. It also has on the premises one of Ullapool's two excellent book shops, and is nowadays being run by the next generation of the family.

Today, the port is used by private yachts, fishing boats, those on local excursions and by the daily Caledonian MacBrayne's passenger and car ferry to Stornoway in the Isle of Lewis. Before it became Cal Mac, David MacBrayne's was the dominant, indeed only, shipping firm of any size in the west coast of Scotland, giving rise to the refrain:

> 'God rules the World
> And all it contains
> Except for the West Highlands
> Which is run by MacBrayne's.'

Geologically, the Ullapool area is spectacular. There is evidence that 1.5 billion years ago the largest bolide (a type of meteor) ever to strike the British Isles hit the Ullapool area with a force of 145,000 megatons, the 30-mile-diameter crater today lying under The Minch. Ullapool is surrounded by rugged, jagged mountains, mainly composed of ancient Torridian sandstone, particularly Beinn Dearg ('red mountain') to the west and An Teallach ('the forge') to the south-west, both rising to around 3,500 feet in an area known locally as the 'Great Wilderness'.

As with most of the Highlands, the Loch Broom and Ullapool area suffered from the distress and hardship caused by The Clearances, when families were evicted, often with the connivance of the clan chief or local laird, to make way for sheep farmers from the Lowlands. James Hogg, the 'Ettrick Shepherd' and author of *Confessions of a Justified Sinner*,(a brilliant post-modern novel written over 100 years before modernism arrived) visited the area in the early 1800s and wrote movingly about the plight of the homeless peasants at the hands of the chief of the local MacKenzie clan.

In the 20th century, Gruinard, a small, one-mile-long island in Gruinard Bay just south of Little Loch Broom, was used by the government as the location for biological wafare and anthrax experiments, and was placed under quarantine for animals and humans. The tests were halted in the early 1980s, and in 1990 the island was officially declared anthrax-free. Visitors are today allowed back on to the island for the first time in almost 50 years, but they do so at their own risk.

Iain recounts a sinister undercurrent to the affair.

Anthrax Island

Rab mentions Gruinard Island and its role as a biological weapons laboratory, contaminated as it was by anthrax spores. Gruinard, just a mile off the West Highland coast, had largely been forgotten by the Great British Public when, in 1981, newspapers and other media organisations started to get communiqués on behalf of something called Dark Harvest, demanding the government decontaminate the place. Dark Harvest claimed to have landed scientists on the island and collected hundreds of pounds of toxic soil.

The group said it would leave samples of that soil at 'appropriate points', which it suggested would end the government's indifference and the public's ignorance of the issue. A sealed package containing anthrax bacilli was left outside the government's military research plant at Porton Down, and within days another was found in Blackpool, where the Conservative Party was holding its annual conference.

I remember, as Highland-based journalists working for the BBC, we tried to track down Dark Harvest. We had a very clear impression where that operation may have been based. But we could never quite prove it, and the identity of Dark Harvest remains a mystery to this day.

Nevertheless, decontamination of the island began in 1986, and by 1990 it was declared anthrax-free. To mark the event – and probably to prove they weren't lying - the Thatcher government sent junior defence minister Michael Neubert out to Gruinard in an open boat. He may not have been very well prepared for the wild West Coast.

A couple of us journalistic types joined him aboard and. as the rain blew in sideways and the minister shivered in a Westminster suit and no coat, one of my colleagues turned to him and asked innocently: 'So, minister. Does this mean you're a Tory wet?' He didn't laugh.

Ullapool is today something of a cultural magnet. There are art, music and dance festivals ('feisean') throughout the year, the most popular being the annual Loopallu (think backwards) Festival, known as 'the Best Little Fest in the West', which was first staged in 2005. Bands and performers who have played the Festival include Mumford & Sons, Saw Doctors, Franz Ferdinand, Paolo Nutini, Echo and the Bunnymen and the Levellers. The population of the town at least doubles during the Festival.

The Ullapool Book Festival takes place every May and the prestigious Guitar Festival tunes up in October. Regular music and dance events take place at the town's McPhail Centre and in bars across the town. Ullapool is also home to the West Highland College, part of the University of the Highlands and Islands, which is located in a large, refurbished herring store in the town.

Ullapool is not normally a town which one would visit in passing, although a visitor would enjoy other interesting places further north, such as Achiltibuie, Lochinver, Kinlochbervie and Cape Wrath (which. by the way, is not a synonym for the English word for 'anger': it derives from the old Norse 'hvarf', or 'turning point', as it marks where the North Sea turns south into The Minch).

Ullapool is certainly worth the hour or so trip by car – there is no rail line – from Inverness, and there is no shortage of accommodation if you book ahead. Which you really should do.

WICK:

THE WEEKERS OF CAITHNESS

The first time I travelled to Wick was from Inverness Airport when I was about five or six years old. In hindsight, the plane looked and felt like a pre-War crop-sprayer, and it bounced and shuddered through a gale-force storm for the entire flight. I was terrified.

To say I was relieved when we bounced unsteadily onto the runway at Wick is a serious understatement. I had stopped trembling only by the time I arrived at my mother's old farmhouse near Lybster a few miles to the south of Wick. So that was my introduction to the capital of Caithness. However, as I grew older, I became fond of Wick: but on my many subsequent visits to Lybster I travelled by road.

The county of Caithness is, in a cultural and linguistic sense, significantly different to the rest of the Scottish Highlands. Due to its location in the extreme north-east of Britain, during early medieval times it was subject to Norwegian rule, and the Gaelic tongue was conspicuous by its virtual absence, except in the far west of the county. The inhabitants mainly spoke 'Norn', a variety of Old Norse, and this influence is still evident in many of the placenames.

The name of the port of Wick, some 15 miles south of John O'Groats on the east coast of Caithness, derives from the Old Norse 'vik', meaning 'bay'. By the 17th century, Old Scots had largely replaced the Caithness Norn dialect, and Wick was called 'Week' or 'Weik'. In Inverness today, the colloquial name for an inhabitant of the town is a 'Weeker' (or 'Dirty Weeker': not for reasons of hygiene but rather a corruption of the Wick dialect word 'dirdie', meaning 'busy').

The town, with a population today of around 7,500, sits on Wick Bay on the estuary of the River Wick. As with many parts of the Highlands, there is evidence of Neolithic and Bronze Age settlement in the area. During the 300 years or so of Norse occupation, which ended with the 1266 Treaty of Perth granting mainland sovereignty to Scotland, Viking longboats and Norse fishing craft made full use of its natural harbour.

The town was also the location of Wick Castle, built by the Norse Earl of Caithness, Haraald Madasson, and this is one of the oldest surviving keeps in Scotland. Since the departure of the Norsemen, it passed through the hands of several worthy families and was finally abandoned by the Dunbars in 1910. All that remains today is a tall tower, known as the 'Old Man of Wick', which is perched on the edge of the cliffs just south of Wick Bay.

Not Such An Old Man

Reference is here made to the Old Man of Wick. You may find many other references on your maps and guide books to other places similarly christened. There's the Old Man of Storr, on Skye, for instance, the Old Man of Stoer in Sutherland, and then, to the north-east, there's the Old Man of Lochnagar (and, no, I'm not talking about the Heir to the Throne). There are many more, and there's a reason.

The reason is not that Highlanders were unhealthily preoccupied with mortality, though some might argue that that is true. If you have the chance, have a look at as many of these places so described and you may notice something they have in common. You may conclude that all are rocky, upthrusting outcrops of one kind or another, because they are. You may wonder how that led to them being christened 'old man'. It didn't. And they weren't.

These placenames were all originally conferred on these places by Gaelic speakers. The word for an old man in Gaelic is 'bodach'. But that's not what the earthy Gael saw when he, or indeed she, looked at them. Like Native Americans an ocean away, they tended to confer names on places that properly represented how they looked. Victorian mapmakers were appropriately scandalised by what they chose.

Let me put it this way. The Gaelic for the male reproductive organ is 'bod', and that's what many of these thrusty places were originally called. So, when the mapmakers came to translate these placenames, in an age when even chesterfield sofa legs had to be covered up – hey presto – a new Gaelic name was conferred on those x-rated place names, and duly translated into English. And so, senility was imposed on the scenery. Now you know what their real names are.

If you're like me, you may be unable to get rid of this knowledge once you have it: but don't tell the children.

For 500 years Wick was the administrative centre of Caithness. King James VI declared the town a Royal Burgh in 1589 but, until the late 18th century, it remained a quiet little market town and herring port. However, during the 19th century Wick underwent a dramatic expansion.

The old town of Wick lies to the north of the bay. Towards the end of the 18th century, Sir William Pulteney and the British Fisheries Society began to develop a harbour on the south side of the bay, partly to provide employment for people who had been evicted during The Clearances. With the assistance of Thomas Telford, who built Wick Bridge to connect Wick to what was now called Pulteney and who constructed a new pier in 1831, work began in 1803 on redeveloping the harbour, and the herring industry took off.

By the time the herring trade peaked in 1900, the number of vessels based in Wick harbour had risen to over 1100 and there were 14,000 people engaged, one way or another, in the herring business. Wick had become the largest herring port in Europe. Indeed, over two particularly busy days, some 50 million herring were landed at the harbour.

However, by the early 20th century over-fishing had begun to exhaust the herring stocks and the port went into relative decline. By 1940, there were only around 30 boats in the harbour, roughly the same number as today, although there are now three harbours as well as an extensive marina for personal and pleasure craft.

The existence of the local Old Pulteney distillery, established in 1826 and still today very much a going concern, no doubt encouraged the efforts of the workforce who at one time were estimated to be consuming 3,000 litres of whisky every week. The distillery is the furthest north on mainland Britain. Its single malts, in particular the 21-year-old which was selected World Whisky of the Year in the *2012 Whisky Bible*, have won gold medals at some of the world's most prestigious tasting events.

Old Pulteney distillery closed in 1930, as the parish of Wick voted in 1922 to ban the sale of alcohol, but the ban only lasted for 25 years and the distillery re-opened in 1951, no doubt to public relief, although the Wee Frees probably weren't too happy. But the Wee Frees are not renowned for their hedonistic *joie de vivre*.

In 1902 Pulteney was merged into the Royal Burgh of Wick. Wick became the more upmarket shopping and residential area, with fine Victorian houses modelled on Bath and designed by Thomas Telford, while Pulteney is the old fishing centre of the town.

A little-known fact about Pulteney, which I am now going to tell you, is that it was the site of the first bomb to be dropped on Britain by the Luftwaffe in World War II. On 1 July 1940, 15 residents, eight of them children, were killed when the bomb landed on Bank Street, one of the oldest streets in the area. Today there still remains the gap where the bomb fell, as a memorial to the loss of life.

In the 1930s, the artist LS Lowry, who often had the good sense to holiday in Caithness, painted the Black Stairs in Pulteney and entitled the work 'The Steps at Wick'. In 2013 the painting was sold at Bonham's auction house for just under £1 million.

Also in Pulteney a specialist glass manufacturer, Caithness Glass, set up business in 1961, and the company gained a worldwide reputation for the quality of its glassware, including the trophy for the BBC 'Mastermind' programme. Glass production, however, later moved south to Perth.

Reeking of History

Wick is a place that feels like the most Caithness of Caithness places. Pultneytown is certainly worth a visit, as a historical milestone. The building of this fisher village marked the move from just a collection of thatched buildings to becoming the centre of commerce in the land of the Cat and the capital of Caithness.

The poet, playwright and all-round author George Gunn says the most resilient thing about the place is the people, who have always managed to make a living and construct an economy. Robert Louis Stevenson, who wrote the odd thing himself, pronounced this 'the baldest of God's coasts'. He should know, as his family constructed so many lighthouses on these inhospitable coasts.

George Gunn says the town 'simply reeks of history'. To find more about what he describes as the people's ingenuity at survival, then the Wick Heritage Centre, bursting with artefacts, is worth a visit. If you want to learn more about the Little World of Caithness, you could do worse than read George Gunn's book The Province of the Cat. Or consult a CD, by another local musician Gordon Gunn, which promises to be a 'Musical Map of Caithness'. I have a reason to recommend it. I'm on it, reading George Gunn's words. And not for the first time.

Modern manufacturing on a vastly greater scale can be found today in the Bridge of Wester area of Wick. The Wester Fabrication Yard is a spin-off from the North Sea oil boom, which has revolutionised, indeed created, so much of today's Highland economy. The Yard produces pipeline bundles, containing all the hi-tech components necessary for subsea oil operation, measuring up to a remarkable 7.7 kilometres in length. These huge structures are then towed offshore to their resting places deep in the North Sea.

Culturally and historically, there is no shortage of places and events to enjoy in Wick and the local area. The Wick Heritage Museum on Bank Street has a range of Wick-related artefacts and archives, including boats and part of a lighthouse. Five miles to the north of the town, Castle Sinclair Girnigoe is a 14th-century, four-storey tower house on a rocky promontory.

Reiss, also to the north, has a fine beach backed onto by Wick Golf Course. The Caithness Broch Centre, again on the road to John O'Groats, is a new arts centre, which tells the story of Caithness from pre-Viking days till the present, and contains models of a Viking settlement and longboat.

Secret Village

As you head up the east coast towards Wick, you will come to a secret village. Dunbeath is almost hidden under the north road and the bridge they built to bypass the place. On your approach, you might not even realise it's a bridge, because the big sweep of this structure rises so precipitously from north to south, you might think you're merely on a hill. But look hard and you'll see traces of the old road, down on the valley floor.

Dunbeath was a fisher town, built to cash in on the herring boom of the early 19th century, when 100 boats plied their trade from here. Many of them were crewed by people who had been cleared from the inland strath nearby: around 80 families in all. If it wasn't to be America, then it was the fishing for you. The harbour's still here, but it's a lot quieter these days, and the herring are gone.

The main thing about Dunbeath, though, is Neil Gunn. Neil M Gunn was born here in 1891. Though he's somewhat out of fashion these days, this was a great writer of the 20th century, with his novel The Silver Darlings – *about the herring – being perhaps best remembered. There's a statue – Kenn and the Salmon – depicting a scene from one of his books down at the harbour. And just about everywhere you wander there's a reminder of one scene or another from his work.*

If you're not familiar with Gunn, then a visit to the Dunbeath Heritage Centre will soon put that right. Installed in the very primary school where Gunn was a pupil, it maps out the Dunbeath River on its floor, and puts the work of the only Zen Nationalist I know of into proper proportion.

And here's how Gunn himself described the places and the boyhood memories it evoked: 'Birches, hazel trees for nutting, pools with trout and an occasionally visible salmon, river-flats with the wind on the bracken and disappearing rabbit scuts, a wealth of wild flower and small bird life, the soaring hawk, the unexpected roe, the ancient graveyard, thoughts of the folk who once lived far inland in straths and hollows, the past and the present held in a moment of day-dream'.

Back at the harbour, there's evidence of some beautiful restoration work – an ice house, a boat house with a restored yawl in it and, just round the corner, a salmon bothy - all work completed by the local Preservation Trust.

Beyond the village, you can wander through hazel woods to an Iron Age broch, which looks out over the broad reaches of the Flow Country, where such household names as snooker's Steve Davis and the band Genesis used to plant trees as a tax dodge, till the government closed that loophole. The trees now belong to other people, and are being chopped down and taken away at the time of writing, restoring the miles of peat bog to their original condition.

I once won a writing award named after Neil Gunn, which is still conferred on much more deserving people to this day, so I am biased. But this is a fascinating hamlet, hazel trees and unexpected roes, all but hidden away beneath the rumble of the A9 traffic.

If your interests include football, Wick Academy FC ('the Scorries') was established in the Pulteney area in 1896 and joined the Highland League in 1994, where recently the club has been prospering. And if all of this is not enough, Wick can also boast ownership of the shortest street in the world: Ebenezer Street, at the end of Mackay's Hotel, is slightly over two metres long and certified as such by the *Guinness Book of Records*.

A few miles south of Wick, just off the A99, is the small hamlet of Whaligoe, where you will find the 'Whaligoe Steps'. In the 19th century it was a landing place for fishing boats, and 365 steps had to be built by hand from the clifftop to the natural harbour below, bypassing the oyster catcher and tern nests on the cliff face. The boats landed, discharged their cargoes of herring, haddock, cod and ling, and groups of women (why is it always women who carry things?) hauled the heavy, full baskets of fish up all these steps to the top, from where they were forwarded to Wick for sale.

The local tourist board has obviously been reading up on its health and safety responsibilities at Whaligoe Steps, as its official pamphlet about this precipitous stairway reads 'Not recommended for wheelchairs'. Thanks for the advice, fellas, although it's tricky enough by foot.

Then there are the fishing, walking and sailing, the trips to John O'Groats (not that there is much to look at), the beautiful sands and headland at Dunnet Bay, the inland Flow Country (the largest expanse of peatland bog in Europe), and much more in this austerely beautiful county.

Caithness is a land of infinite variety, although you shouldn't look forward to mountain climbing, as there aren't any, unless you count the 2,300-feet Morven in the far south of the county. Nor is Wick the warmest town in Britain and it can be windy, but its latitude should tell you that. It's a fascinating place. And the airport is perfectly safe.

THE SOUTH-WEST HIGHLANDS

Now that you've read and, we hope, enjoyed this book, a question that might occur to you is: where's the rest of the Highlands and Islands? It's a fair question.

Yes, there are many more places we could have written about, but then you'd be in the excess baggage zone, weighed down by a mighty volume that would take you a very long time to read. And with an awful lot of places to choose.

When we began *Where Seagulls Dare*, we made a decision to concentrate on Inverness, the Great Glen (at least as far south as Fort Augustus) and the North. Several parts of the North are, in our view, not as well known as they deserve, and we aimed to address this imbalance. The emergence of the North Coast 500 marketing campaign may also do this, though it's not entirely uncontroversial.

Nonetheless, we are very aware there's a lot more to the Highlands than what's contained between these covers. At the moment, we're actively planning a second book, when our seagulls will be flying southwards, with a greater degree of confidence. But. for now, here are a few of our personal highlights from these areas, should you wish to go further afield, and which will feature in the forthcoming companion volume.

Badenoch and Strathspey: For many people, the village of **Aviemore**, the centre of the winter sports industry, is not really for them. Billy Connolly, having played a gig there many years ago, branded it 'Colditz wi' windies', but that's a bit unkind. The development of this place, in the shadow of the Cairngorms, really began in the 1960s when the Council drove a road in there off the old A9. Reo Stakis then began building.

Yes, the *Aviemore Centre*, owned these days by Macdonald Hotels, does still resemble what it is: a 1960s-70s concrete lego kit of unprepossessingly square buildings, surrounded by car parks. But you should have seen what it looked like before. There have been several attempts to make it more visually appealing, and some have even succeeded.

But there are bits worth visiting away from the Centre, too. *The Cairngorm Hotel* serves good grub and boasts an atmospheric interior. There are lots of shops selling outdoor gear. Up the road, there's the *Coylum Bridge Hotel*, which boasts loads of room, a swimming pool complex and is a family holiday all under one roof, if you fancy that kind of thing.

And a little further away, we recommend the *Rothiemurchus Estate*. They make much of their green credentials in one of the most beautiful parts of Scotland, and again they target families, as well as the individual hillwalker, climber, canoeist, four-by-four off-roader, gorge walker, mountain biker and archer. Yes, archer.

Then there's The Hill, aka *CairnGorm Mountain*. Up there, the funicular railway, constructed at a cost of several millions, will take you high into the mountains, summer and winter. There's ski-ing and snowboarding, après-ski entertainment and much more.

Elsewhere in what should NEVER be called the Spey Valley (but regrettably is, especially by the tourist trade), because that's what Strathspey means, there are many attractions: there's the steam railway at **Boat of Garten**, itself a bonny little place; there's the *Highland Wildlife Park* at **Kincraig**, which features Siberian tigers, Polar bears, which they're presently hoping to breed with more success than Edinburgh Zoo has with its pandas, and snow monkeys, which have very red bums, and would undoubtedly look good on the dance floor; and there's *Landmark*, in the peaceful and pretty village of **Carrbridge** (where one of your authors once tried to drown himself), another family-focused place where you can take a treetop walk, skydive on slides and rides and they're building a Butterfly House soon, which sounds ace.

And top of the Trip Advisor Pops of late is the *Highland Folk Museum* in the village of **Newtonmore**. The name may sound dull, but in fact it's an open-air historical village featuring over 30 buildings from different Highland eras. The site is a mile long, with a 1700s township (featuring six houses) at one end, through to a 1930s working croft at the other. They've transported some of these buildings from elsewhere, then reassembled them on site. There's a café, a vintage sweet shop a children's playground, and staff all dressed for the part. In the school house, you may get chastised for your hand writing. And they don't charge you to get in.

There's more, as Jimmy Cricket the comedian once said, but you'll have to wait for it....

Going west, there's **Lochaber**, where you can find another ski development at Aonach Mor, trading as *Nevis Range*, where they are equally keen on all-year-round adventure on the slopes next to Britain's highest mountain. And, of course, they have Britain's only mountain gondola, which will transport you around 2,000 feet up the mountain, where you can disembark and – depending on the season, and your taste – ski back down in winter or wander off into the environment in the summer. Wouldn't advise it the other way round.

Like Inverness further north, **Fort William** has its commercial sector, which in this case tends to major on tartans, woollens and mountain gear. Like Inverness, it's a great base for heading out to lots of other places. There's the overpowering and still melancholy **Glencoe**, where the Macdonalds were massacred and where Jimmy Savile used to have a (now boarded-up) home. Great climbing and a good pub are to be found here.

Ben Nevis, and **Glen Nevis** at the foot of the mountain, are natural magnets for the adventurous, and there is actually a so-called path up the mountain. But it can be fairly hard going and it is not a climb you should ever consider tackling in t-shirt and trainers. Some people do, and have to be carried off the hill. If they're lucky.

Heading out from the Fort ('an Gearasdan' in the Gaelic: it translates as 'the Garrison') you could go west: in fact, just as far west as you can go on mainland Britain. The **Ardnamurchan Peninsula**, all craggy mountains, empty glens and wild moorland, gives way to white beaches and sparkling water. There is abundant wildlife in this Cleared quarter and stunning views, on a good day, out to the islands of Skye and Mull. **Strontian**, after which they named strontium, an 'earth metal' discovered there and which was once used in sugar production, then in cathode ray tubes for television sets, is a village worth visiting.

If you choose to take to the **Road to the Isles**, departing westwards from **Corpach**, you will pass the *Outward Bound Locheil Centre* and a spot in the loch where they farm mussels. That's if you're driving. The alternative could be the *Jacobite Steam Train* heading up the coast, which is as romantic as it sounds. On the way, you will cross Harry Potter's bridge. The *Glenfinnan Viaduct* is the spectacular construction over which the train to Hogwarts crosses in the films, and it won't disappoint, whether you see it from a carriage or a car.

The Road to the Isles will take you through some of the most spectacular scenery in the Highlands and eventually deposit you at the busy, if not exactly beautiful, fishing village of **Mallaig**, which is great fun in the summer, and which has a ferry link to **Lochboisdale** in South Uist, at least for summer 2016. The rail journey along the last leg of the *West Highland Line* features regularly in great Railway Journeys of the World, because it is. That simple.

South from here there's **Argyll** (in modern Gaelic: 'Earra-Ghàidheal'). This was once the seat of power in ancient Scotland, the kingdom of Dalriada, or Dal Riata, which also took in a large chunk of northern Ireland. If you turned a map of Scotland sideways, you might see why this made perfect sense, especially to a sea-going people.

It might also explain how, even in the present day, the Gaelic spoken in **Tiree**, almost halfway between Ireland and Scotland sounds to Scottish Gaelic ears very like Irish which, in case you doubted it, is a different language.

Argyll and the Isles today boasts over 3,000 miles of coastline (roughly the same as all of France), 25 inhabited islands, 60 castles and 14 big distilleries. Much of it is also stunningly beautiful.

Just a few highlights then. **Oban** is the main ferry port to the Argyll islands and, until recently beyond to the Western Isles. A strange mixture of the kitsch and the classic, very busy in the summer months with tourists from all airts, it is still capable of bringing you up short with a stunning view as you turn a corner or negotiate a hill. There are pubs for all tastes, from the sophisticated to the couthy to the frankly quite rough. There are hotels a plenty. There's a fish and seafood restaurant in a converted public loo, which is just great. Fish and chips just about anywhere round here are fantastic.

And then there's *McCaig's Folly*, a ring of Bonawe granite looking down on the town. It was built in the late 19th and early 20th century. It was intended to resemble the Colosseum. It was built by a banker. This is not rhyming slang, though he had intended statues of himself and his family to be erected inside it, as well as a central tower, along with a museum and art gallery. When the banker died – and yes, his name was McCaig - building work stopped. Now, there's a garden inside the walls, and people occasionally get married there.

Offshore, there are islands. **Kerrera** is five miles by two, and you can travel there by boat and cycle and walk to your heart's good health. **Lismore** is another like it. Further south, there are the 'Slate Islands', so called because their now defunct quarries once produced millions of slates every year for houses across half the country and beyond.

These slates – they lie around everywhere – come in handy on **Easdale** Island, where they hold the *World Stone Skimming Championships* every September or so (hey, this is the West Highlands: we don't do precise). There are various categories, but the senior prizes are awarded to the top Old Tossers. Honest. To get there, you have to press the button in the ferry shed on the mainland side.

Next door to Easdale is 'Seil Island' which boasts the 'bridge over the Atlantic', a picturesque little hump-backed construction, but it technically does span the ocean. The island of **Luing** is another place just a short ferry trip away, and there they have the *Atlantic Islands Centre*.

The island of **Mull** is one of the biggest islands round here. Once known as the 'Officer's Mess', because of the number of retired military gents who settled there, it's another of those 'Scotland In Miniature' places. There are looming mountains, ruined castles and beautiful white beaches. There's *Duart Castle*, a 13th-century fortress on a rocky promontory. There are white-tailed eagles.

And there's **Tobermory** where multi-coloured, brightly painted houses cluster round one of the most beautiful fishing ports in Scotland. This is the home of the BBC Scotland children's TV series 'Balamory'. So it's kind of cute and kind of couthy. But it also knows how to party, and there are some ace musicians, traditional and modern, hereabouts... not least a one-man music industry called Colin MacIntyre, descended from a distinguished line of Mullachs, who rejoices in the on-the-record name of the Mull Historical Society. He's also just published his first award-winning novel.

Another short ferry hop away is **Iona**, the island where St Columba set up home around 563 AD and where today the multi-faith Iona Community continues to prosper. Locals may scoff – and sometimes they do – but it really does have a special atmosphere. Among those buried in the island's church yard are various kings of Scotland and John Smith, probably the best Prime Minister the Labour Party never had. And a damn good man, whatever your politics.

Further off Mull is the island of **Staffa**, five miles to the south-west. The name means 'pillar island' in Old Norse, and you can charter a boat passage here to sail into the vast sea cave of basalt columns: **Fingal's Cave**. Its fame spread far and wide in the 19th century and Queen Victoria came to see. So did a bloke called Mendelssohn. He wrote his Hebrides Overture after that visit.

There's much more to Argyll, but we'll go south now to **Kintyre**: a long finger pointing accusingly south to Ireland. The west coast beaches are beautiful and pounded by the Atlantic waves. Surfers come here. So did Paul McCartney, and the ex-Beatle wrote his chart-topping 'Mull of Kintyre' while living here. **Saddell Beach** is where they shot the video, pipe band and all.

Finally, there's the **Southern Isles**. Starting with watery but warm-hearted **North Uist** (though it's not strictly southern), we will, when we get there, transport you across the great religious divide to **South Uist** where Our Lady shrines appear and where, again, the locals run the place. Further south, and on to **Vatersay** and beautiful **Barra**, where the plane still lands on the beach in a small plume of spray. It was once Scotland's entry in a competition to find the most beautiful island in the world. Barrachs were not surprised by that, because they knew already.

These are just some of the places where seagulls will dare next. Lucky seagulls.

Index of Placenames

(This Index contains the Highlands and Islands placenames mentioned in the text. Page numbers in bold italic indicate they are one of the 25 areas featured in the book.)